Vegan Success

Scrumptious, Healthy Vegan Recipes for Busy People

Susan C. Daffron
& James H. Byrd

Logical Expressions, Inc.
http://www.logicalexpressions.com

ISBN-13: 978-0-9749245-1-9
ISBN-10: 0-9749245-1-2

Library of Congress Control Number: 2006907834

Warning and disclaimer: This book is designed to provide information about vegetarian cooking. Every effort has been made to make it as complete and accurate as possible, but no warranty or fitness is implied.

The information in this book is provided on an "as is" basis. Logical Expressions, Inc. and the authors take no responsibility for any errors or omissions. The author and Logical Expressions, Inc. also shall have no responsibility to any person or entity with respect to loss or damages arising from information contained in this book or from any programs or documents that may accompany it.

Contents

On Being Vegan

A "vegan" is someone who eats **no** animal products of any kind. Obviously, it means steak is not for dinner, but it also means no milk, cheese, eggs, meat, poultry, or fish are on the menu either. The bottom line is that if the food had a face, or if it came from something that had a face, vegans don't eat it.

My husband James and I have been vegan since 1994. Unlike many vegans who have political or ethical reasons for not eating animal products, we became vegan for a far more mundane reason: our health.

Back in 1994, James and I read a book called *Fit for Life* by Harvey and Marilyn Diamond. The book actually isn't about being a vegetarian at all, let alone taking the drastic step of becoming vegan. It's about how to eat foods in the right combinations to lose weight. Concepts like "food combining" and "natural hygiene" are not new. We heard about them, but didn't try them because it all seemed so complicated.

After reading *Fit For Life*, we realized that the principles of food combining are actually easy if you don't eat animal products. So we decided to try the *Fit for Life* eating methods for one week using a vegan approach. We felt so much better that we never stopped!

James and I are busy people, so being vegan had to fit into our lifestyle. We run our own company, Logical Expressions, Inc., so we work long hours. Even though our schedules can be hectic, we share cooking responsibilities. I cook three days a week, James does three days, and we trade off Wednesdays.

We both manage to create home-cooked meals without putting a strain on our nerves or resorting to processed convenience foods.

Because, we live about 20 miles from the nearest town, we can't just run to the corner store or get pizza (or any other food) delivered. If we're hungry, we have to make dinner ourselves. Like everyone else, we are faced with that eternal question, "what's for dinner?" The less you feel like cooking, the more challenging the question becomes.

Over the years, after people find out we are vegan and discover all the things we *don't* eat, these folks then wonder what we *do* eat. Because so many people have asked us this question, we decided to write a book with a number of our favorite easy recipes, many of which we make all the time. In this book, we focus on how you can create simple, unfussy, goof proof food quickly and easily.

Because neither of us are trained chefs, these recipes require no gourmet techniques or special skills beyond the most rudimentary kitchen competence. If you can chop up veggies, saute stuff in a skillet, or throw things into a pot, you can make these recipes. You'll also find that the recipes are big on flavor and satisfy the biggest hunger.

Anyone who has lived with a vegan knows that a hungry vegan can power down a lot of food. If you're eating unprocessed foods, such as vegetables and grains, you can eat a lot and not gain weight.

Of course, technically, a vegan can eat just as badly as anyone else, since French fries and some chocolates can be construed as vegan. But as a general rule, it's much easier for vegans to stay slim because even when our recipes use margarines or oils, they are generally far less fatty than similar recipes made with animal products.

If you are new to vegan cooking, or find yourself cooking for a vegan in the family, this book will make your life easier. Enjoy!

Susan Daffron & James Byrd

Vegan Glossary

Certain foods in this book may be unfamiliar to you if you haven't done much vegetarian cooking. This glossary gives you definitions for some of the more unusual ingredients you may find in this book or other vegetarian cookbooks.

Agar-Agar - Sometimes called just "agar" this gelling agent is most often sold as flakes. Unlike gelatin, it is made from a sea vegetable so it is vegan.

Arrowroot - This white powder looks a lot like cornstarch and is used in much the same way as a thickener. However, arrowroot tends to create a more "glaze-like" quality to sauces. You should dissolve it in cold water before adding to a sauce, so it doesn't form clumps.

Brewer's/Nutritional Yeast - Unlike other yeasts, this yeast is not used for baking bread. However, these powdery yellow flakes can be a great source of vitamin B-12. Red Star's Vegetarian Support Formula (T6635+) brand for example, is fortified with B vitamins. Nutritional yeast imparts a mildly "cheesy" flavor and color, so it's often used in vegan recipes. You often can find it in the bulk food area of grocery/ health food stores.

Bragg's Liquid Aminos - Used like soy sauce, Bragg's is a lower salt condiment with a slightly different flavor.

Chinese Five Spice - This blend of five spices includes cinnamon, cloves, fennel seeds, star anise, and Szechwan peppercorns. Most well stocked grocery stores have it. Health food and Asian markets almost always do.

Egg Replacer - This powder is made from starches and acts as binding agent in baking. Ener-G Egg Replacer is widely available in both grocery and health food stores.

Miso - This paste is made from fermented soybeans. It imparts a salty rich taste to soups and sauces; however, you should only add it at the end of the recipe because boiling destroys the enzymes. You can buy miso in different colors that range from light to dark. The darker the miso, the saltier it is. Most misos need to be refrigerated.

Sesame Oil - This oil is made from sesame seeds and comes in two types. The light colored one is used for dressings and frying. However, the darker Asian sesame oil has a strong taste and fragrance, so you should use it sparingly for flavor.

Soy Sauce/Tamari - Most people who have been to Asian restaurants are familiar with soy sauce, which is made from fermented soybeans and sometimes wheat. Shoyu soy sauce generally contains wheat, whereas tamari soy sauce does not. Unfortunately, not all companies strictly follow the terminology, so if you need to avoid wheat products, read the label.

Tahini (Sesame Paste) - This paste is made from sesame seeds, much like peanut butter is made from peanuts. Like natural peanut butter, you need to stir tahini before using it to blend in the oils, which tend to separate in the jar.

Tempeh - In recipes, tempeh often stands in for meat because it has a chewy consistency. It is made from fermented soy protein and has been a staple food in Indonesia for literally centuries. The soybeans and grains are cooked and then inoculated with a culture called rhizopus oligosporus. Although virtually all tempeh has a somewhat nutty flavor, some tempeh also is mixed with grains, which can change the flavor somewhat.

Tofu - Like soymilk and tempeh, tofu is made from soybeans. However, tofu is processed with some type of coagulating agent such as nigari or calcium sulfate. You can buy two basic types of tofu. Fresh tofu is packed in water and needs to be refrigerated. Aseptic or "silken" tofu is vacuum packed, so it does not need to be refrigerated until you open it. Tofu comes in various textures that range from soft to extra firm. Firm tofus can be cubed and added to stir-fries. Silken tofus are often blended and turned into sauces or added to soups. For even more convenience, some stores carry baked tofus that are precooked and marinated. All you have to do it cut it up and throw it in the pan.

Udon - These Japanese noodles are made from wheat flour instead of semolina. Most natural food stores carry udon noodles.

Vegan Shopping List - Naming the Names

Over the years, we've tried a lot of different vegetarian-oriented products. Just because it's "vegetarian" or "heath food" doesn't mean it has to taste bland, strange or just plain bad. (Although let's face it, some soy cheeses taste like old gym socks.)

Many cookbooks won't tell you which of the many brands out there in vegan-ville actually taste good. So here are our recommendations for various vegetarian products that have passed our taste test. We also give you a few hints on what to look for (and avoid) when selecting a given type of product.

Although in the recipes we use generic terms such as soy milk or vegan margarine, the products listed below are the ones we actually use when we make the recipes ourselves. Most of them are widely available in health food stores and even some traditional grocery stores in the United States. However, if you can't find these particular brands, don't feel bad. Vegan products are getting better all the time, so you may find new brands that you like even better than these!

Bouillon Cubes - Hugli, Morga. Look for ones with no mystery additives like "natural flavors."

Canned Beans - Eden (http://www.edenfoods.com) or Westbrae (http:// www.westbrae.com). Look for organically grown beans packed in water. Some also include Kombu, which is okay. (Kombu is a sea vegetable, if you're wondering.)

Canned Tomatoes and Ketchup - Muir Glen (http://www.muirglen. com). Look for tomato products made with organic tomatoes.

Cheese Slices - Tofutti (http://www.tofutti.com). Sadly, Tofutti changed their "block" cheeses, but the slices are still okay. Many cheeses are not vegan; watch out for "casein" on the label.

Coconut Milk - Thai Kitchen (http://www.thaikitchen.com). Look for coconut milk without any preservatives. Don't bother with "Lite" coconut milk; all you're paying for is extra water.

Cream Cheese and Sour Cream - Tofutti (http://www.tofutti.com). Nothing else comes close. Beware of some seriously nasty imitators.

Egg Replacer - Ener-G (http://www.ener-g.com). Virtually the only one we've ever seen; it works great and one box will last you a long, long time.

Extra Virgin Olive Oil - Bertolli (http://www.bertolli.com). Look for cold pressed extra virgin olive oil. It's worth the extra money.

"Fake Meat" Products - Yves (http://www.yvesveggie.com). We're especially fond of the Veggie Ground Round. Other fake hamburgers add extra spices, such as chili spices, which makes them less versatile in cooking.

Ice Cream - So Delicious (http://www.turtlemountain.com). After years of eating no ice cream or less-than-tasty rice-based versions, So Delicious was a revelation. Even non-vegans love this stuff.

Ice Cream Sandwiches - Tofutti Cuties (http://www.tofutti.com). Beware, they are totally addictive!

Long Grain and Wild Rice, Rice Pilaf, Couscous - Near East (http://www.neareast.com). Yes, it's more expensive than buying plain rice, but sometimes it's worth it for the convenience factor.

Mayonnaise - Vegenaise (http://www.followyourheart.com). You'll find it in the refrigerated section. Unfortunately, strange-tasting mayonnaises abound, but this one is great and tastes like *real* mayo.

Nutritional Yeast (Brewer's yeast) - Red Star's Vegetarian Support Formula (T6635+) is fortified with Vitamin B12.

Oils - Hain, Spectrum Organics (http://www.spectrumorganics.com). In general look for "first cold pressing" or cold pressed.

Salsa - Pace Picante sauce (http://www.pacefoods.com). We like medium, but we like spicy food, so your mileage may vary.

Soy Milk - Vitasoy Original Plain (http://www.vitasoy-usa.com). For cooking, look for mild-tasting soymilk.

Spices - Frontier (http://www.frontiercoop.com). Look for non-irradiated spices.

Tahini and Nut Butters - Maranatha Natural Foods (http://www.nspiredfoods.com). Opt for non-roasted varieties, which are less acidic and more versatile for cooking.

Tamari - San-J (http://www.san-j.com). Look for low sodium tamari soy sauce.

Tempeh - Turtle Island (http://www.tofurky.com). Try and find one made with organically grown soybeans. We like the five-grain Turtle Island the best (in the green package).

Tofu (Silken/Aseptic) - Mori Nu (http://www.morinu.com). This type of tofu is actually not refrigerated, so you may find it mixed in with pantry-type items at the store.

Tofu (Regular) - Island Spring (http://www.islandspring.com) or Small Planet (http://www.smallplanettofu.com). Look for tofu made with organically grown soybeans.

Tofu Scrambler, Hummus, Tofu Burger - Fantastic Foods (http://www.fantasticfoods.com).

Vegan Margarine - Earth Balance (http://www.earthbalance.net). Look for margarine with no trans fats.

Veggie "Chicken" and "Beef" Broth - Abco is a brand we've used, but we've only been able to get it in bulk, so it may be hard to find. Other brands exist, just check to make sure the broth is really vegan; many aren't.

Reading Labels

Many vegans spend a lot of time reading labels. In general, we try to look for items with as few ingredients as possible. I once got into a pointless discussion with someone who didn't understand why I didn't want to ingest anything containing ingredients I didn't recognize. The person I was talking to was extolling the virtues of a lactose-free "milk" product. Instead of opting for soymilk, which contains just soybeans and water, he was drinking a product with a chemical-laden ingredients list that was five inches long. Yuck!

While you're reading labels, even in health food stores, you may run across quite a few ingredients that are not vegan. Here are a few non-vegan "vegetarian" ingredients to watch out for:

Albumin - egg whites.

Casein - milk proteins from cheese (often found in "non-dairy" products). Note that many vegetarian cheeses are ***not*** vegan.

Rennet/Rennin - animal product used to coagulate cheese.

Gelatin - derived from animal products.

Lactose - milk sugar (as opposed to lactic acid, which is not derived from dairy).

Lard/suet/animal shortening/cholesterol/tallow - made from rendered animal parts.

Whey - the liquid that remains when casein is removed from milk.

"Natural Flavors" - this catchall term may be fine or may be hiding some spices or flavorings that are based on animal products. You may need to ask the manufacturer.

Strict vegans may also not want to eat honey, which is an insect product that is used as a sweetener. (This book does include honey in a few recipes, but you can easily substitute another sweetener.)

Faking It

Many of us have recipes that we remember from our childhood, along with a lot of non-vegan cookbooks left over from our non-veg life. For example, Toll House cookies using the recipe on the back of Nestle's chocolate chips are one of the most marvelous things in the world (incidentally, dark chocolate often is vegan). It's easy to recreate this recipe using vegan margarine and egg replacer. The vegan version cookies really do taste just as good as the "real" ones.

If you miss recipes from days gone by, all is not lost. Given the wide array of vegan products these days, you can fake many traditional recipes using the hints below. Only a few things are really challenging to "vegan-ize," and they mostly involve egg whites. (So far, we have found nothing that can replace whipped egg whites, so our quest for a vegan soufflé remains unfulfilled.)

With that said, after a while, you can learn to read a recipe and mentally make vegan substitutions. One small vegan victory was when we made a vegan version of Susan's mom's hamburger pie recipe that was cut out of a Canadian magazine in the early 1960s. The vegan version tasted very similar. Even Mom thought so!

Ricotta cheese - mashed tofu mixed with a little vegan mayonnaise.

Milk - Soymilk.

Cream Cheese - vegan cream cheese. (Vegan cheesecakes are a reality!)

Yogurt or **Sour Cream** - soy yogurt and sour cream.

Ground Beef - veggie ground round, tempeh.

Ice Cream - soy ice cream.

Eggs in Baking - egg replacer.

Savory Sauces, Salad Dressings, and Real Gravy

In vegan cooking, it's helpful to learn how to make sauces for vegetables, pastas, and grains. A simple plate of steamed broccoli can undergo a complete makeover, depending on the type of sauce you add to it. Sauces add a lot of variety to vegan menus, so try your hand at these sauces, then experiment with your own variations.

The sauce you make may be hot or cold, highly spiced, subtly herbal, or enlivened by citrus, vinegar, or wine. With the right sauce, your dish can become Far Eastern, Middle Eastern, Mediterranean, or Eastern European.

In this chapter, we reveal our recipe for what we call "Real Gravy." This rich sauce looks, tastes, and smells just like what you think of when someone says "gravy." In other words, it's a thick, savory brown sauce that demands hot mashed potatoes or biscuits fresh from the oven. Yum!

Real Gravy

About 2 cups of gravy. Servings vary, depending on how much gravy you like

This gravy is wonderful because it tastes like real gravy. Really. It's also not hard to make. Pour it on anything you like.

It's especially delicious on the Quick Vegan Stuffing or Vegan Biscuits. You could also serve it on Chicken Fried Tofu Cutlets (page 158), Meet Loaf (page 160), or Veganburgers (page 162).

The "jar" method of mixing the flour with the liquids may seem a little odd to traditional cooks. If you try it just once, you'll be impressed with the time and effort you save. You might even adopt it as your favorite easy mixing method!

If you're a mushroom lover, try adding ½ cup of chopped sautéed mushrooms to the gravy. Chopped onions, cooked until they're soft and caramelized, are another great addition.

Ingredients

¾ cups water

2 tablespoons flour

1 tablespoon tahini

¼ cup soy milk

2 tablespoons vegan margarine

1 teaspoon dried Italian Seasoning

½ teaspoon garlic salt

1 vegan bouillon cube or 2 tablespoons vegan broth powder

¼ teaspoon coriander

1 teaspoon nutritional yeast

Salt and pepper

1. Combine the water, flour, and tahini in a small jar. Shake vigorously until the tahini dissolves.

2. Empty the jar into a small sauce pan.

3. Add the remaining ingredients.

4. Heat over medium heat, stirring occasionally, until the gravy thickens. Add salt and pepper to taste (the amount of salt depends on the saltiness of the bouillon or broth powder you use).

5. Serve nice and hot.

Rich And Hearty Vegan Tomato Sauce

About 3 quarts of sauce.

This unorthodox method produces an incredibly rich, thick sauce that just oozes with tomato flavor. The key ingredients are the olive oil, broth powder, and margarine. Each ingredient contributes extra rich flavor. You could make a very good lower fat sauce by reducing the quantities of oil and margarine, but you won't get quite the same result.

Best of all, you just throw everything into a pot, and aside from stirring it once in a while, you do nothing until the blender phase. You don't need any exotic ingredients, just your basic onion, garlic, and pantry goods. This recipe makes a lot of sauce, but don't worry, it freezes well. You'll be glad you made so much because it's versatile.

For example, you might plop some on top of tofu cutlets, grilled eggplant slices, roasted portabello mushrooms, or on any shape or size of pasta. Use it for pizza or calzones. Or you can stir some into steamed vegetables, drizzle it on a baked potato, or add a little to soups and sauces. For a heavenly snack, heat ½ cup of sauce with a generous shake of dried red pepper flakes, and use it as a dipping sauce for crusty bread or warmed pitas.

Ingredients

4 tablespoons extra virgin olive oil

2 medium onions, chopped

½ cup water

4 cloves garlic, chopped

4 28-ounce cans whole tomatoes in juice

4 15-ounce cans stewed tomatoes

1 teaspoon dried oregano

1 teaspoon dried basil

2 teaspoons dried parsley flakes

5 tablespoons vegan broth powder (chicken is preferable, but veggie or beef flavor will also work)

4 tablespoons vegan margarine

1. Heat the olive oil in a large Dutch oven or stock pot. Add the onions and cook over medium heat, stirring once in a while, until they begin to get soft but not brown (about 8 minutes). Add the water and the garlic. Continue cooking for another 5 minutes.

2. Now dump in all the canned tomatoes with their juice, the herbs, and the broth powder. Stir with a wooden spoon, breaking up the tomatoes just a little.

3. Bring to a simmer, then turn the heat down to medium low, cover partially, and let the sauce cook for anywhere from 45 minutes to an hour, until the tomatoes start to disintegrate. Take a peek periodically, and give it a stir, to make sure nothing sticks to the bottom of the pot.

4. Once everything looks nice and mushy, stir in the margarine until it's incorporated into the sauce.

5. Take the pot off the heat, and let the sauce sit until it's no longer too hot to work with.

6. Now get your blender or food processor out, along with some freezer containers. Blend the sauce, a couple of cups at a time, until it's smooth. Fill a container, then blend another batch. Repeat the process, until you're done.

7. This sauce can be frozen for up to 4 months.

Vegan Hollandaise

About 1 ½ cups.

This is a variation on a recipe that has been circulating in vegetarian and vegan circles for many years. I don't know the origin of it, but I first saw a version in a book called *Vegan Vittles*. We're including it here because it is worth trying on almost any type of steamed or baked vegetable.

Don't try to make this dish with water-packed tofu. You want to use the silken variety that comes in aseptic packages because it blends better. Whatever you do, don't let this sauce boil. If you do, the oil separates, leaving you with an unattractive sauce.

For a nice variation, add 1-2 tablespoons well-drained capers and serve over any steamed green vegetable.

Ingredients

    8 ounces firm silken tofu (full fat variety)

    ¼ cup bland oil, such as canola or safflower

    ¼ cup fresh lemon juice

    ½ teaspoon honey

    ½ teaspoon sea salt

    pinch of white pepper

1. Put all the ingredients in a blender or food processor, and blend until everything is smooth and creamy. You can make this sauce up to 4 hours ahead of time, but no longer because the lemon juice tends to get acidic and lose its fresh taste.

2. Before serving, place the sauce in a double boiler, cover, and heat until it is hot, stirring occasionally.

Japanese Miso Sauce

About 1 ½ cups.

This sauce is very versatile and features a Far East flavor. Serve hot, cold, or at room temperature over vegetables, rice, or udon noodles. You can thin the sauce with a little plain soy milk and serve it over salad greens as a dressing. Or you can even use it as a dip for raw vegetables or your favorite chips.

Ingredients

> 1 package firm silken tofu (full fat variety)
>
> 3 tablespoons plain rice wine vinegar
>
> 2 tablespoons yellow or white miso
>
> 1 tablespoon oil (canola or safflower)
>
> 2 teaspoons honey
>
> 1 teaspoon dark sesame oil
>
> ½ teaspoon coriander
>
> ⅛ teaspoon cayenne
>
> 1 teaspoon tamari
>
> 2 tablespoons nutritional yeast

1. Put all the ingredients into a blender or food processor, and mix until smooth and creamy. Store, refrigerated, up to 5 days.

2. If you wish to serve this sauce hot, do not let it boil. You'll destroy the enzymes in the miso, and it will taste somewhat flat.

Vegan Tartar Sauce

About 1 cup.

Serve this with Chicken Fried Tofu Cutlets (page 158), and French fries for a vegan version of fish and chips.

Ingredients

  1 cup Vegan Mayonnaise (page 135), Tofu Mayonnaise (page 136), or other vegan mayonnaise

  3 tablespoons sweet pickle relish

  1 tablespoon flat leaf parsley, chopped very fine

  1 teaspoon Dijon mustard

1. Mix all the ingredients thoroughly. Taste, and add a little sea salt if needed.

2. Store in a clean glass jar. The sauce can be refrigerated for up to five days.

Creamy Italian Dressing

A little over 1 cup.

This recipe offers the old, familiar taste of Italian dressing. If you like creamy garlic dressing, add two or more cloves of minced fresh garlic.

Ingredients

    1 box firm silken tofu

    2 tablespoons mildly flavored oil, such as canola or safflower

    2 tablespoons red wine vinegar or balsamic vinegar

    1 teaspoon sea salt

    ½ teaspoon dried oregano

    ½ teaspoon dried basil

    ½ teaspoon ground black pepper

1. Put everything in the blender or food processor, and blend until smooth. This sauce can be refrigerated for up to five days.

Thai Peanut Sauce

About 2 cups.

Our local Thai restaurant makes a version of this sauce. They serve it piping hot, on top of deep fried tofu cubes nestled in a bed of fresh steamed spinach. Heavenly!

You can make this sauce with plain soy milk or coconut milk. Soy milk gives you more protein, but you can only store the sauce for a few days. If you make the sauce with coconut milk, it keeps a week or more.

You may have to adjust the flavorings in this sauce a little bit because peanut butters vary enormously in their saltiness and sweetness. In general, if you use the standard commercial peanut butter, you will need less honey. If you use an all natural or organic peanut butter, you may need quite a bit of honey and perhaps some extra tamari.

You can serve this sauce on tofu, tempeh, noodles, rice, or potatoes. Or you could pour it over steamed broccoli, cauliflower, green beans, sugar snap peas, or spinach. If you prefer, you also can chill the sauce and use it as a dip for raw vegetables.

If you like a spicier sauce, add a tablespoon or so of Tabasco or, if you can get it, hot garlic chili paste (which is available in the Asian section of most supermarkets and in some natural foods stores).

Ingredients

   1-½ cups plain soy milk or coconut milk

   ⅔ cup smooth natural peanut butter

   3 tablespoons fresh lime juice

   ¼ cup tamari

   ½ teaspoon crushed red pepper

   ½ teaspoon garlic granules

   1 tablespoon honey or brown sugar (or more to taste)

1. Place everything in a blender and blend until very smooth.

2. Taste, and if the sauce is too sweet, add more soy or coconut milk. If too salty, add a touch of honey and soy milk.

3. Store in a glass container in the refrigerator. To serve hot, heat in a saucepan or microwave. Do not boil.

Thousand Island Dressing

About 1 ½ cups.

If you get a craving every so often for that good old slightly sweet, pickle-flavored Thousand Island dressing, here's one without any scary ingredients.

Don't forget this dressing when you're having Veganburgers (page 162). You can easily simulate a fast food burger "special sauce" by piling on this dressing.

Ingredients

8 ounces firm tofu (water packed is fine; it works better in this dressing than silken tofu)

½ cup ketchup

2 tablespoons mildly flavored oil, like canola or safflower

½ teaspoon dried chives

¼ teaspoon sea salt

¼ teaspoon garlic powder

1 tablespoon fresh parsley, chopped

4 tablespoons sweet pickle relish

2 tablespoons chopped pimento stuffed green olives

1. Combine the tofu, ketchup, oil, chives, sea salt, garlic powder, and parsley in a blender or food processor, and blend until smooth.

2. Mix in the pickle relish and olives. Refrigerate a few hours before serving. This dressing keeps up to 5 days.

Mild Sesame Peanut Dressing

Makes about 2 cups.

This dressing is not just for lettuce. You can use it for a killer spinach salad, an unusual pasta salad, or as a dressing for steamed broccoli or asparagus.

As with the Thai Peanut Sauce (page 20), you may have to adjust the amounts of honey, lime, vinegar, and tamari up or down because peanut butters vary in their sweetness and saltiness. In general, all-natural peanut butters are not as sweet as ordinary versions, so don't be afraid to add more honey. The dressing should be about equal in sweet and tart flavors, with a strong peanut taste.

Ingredients

> 1 cup smooth peanut butter
>
> 2 tablespoons dark sesame oil
>
> 2 tablespoons tahini paste
>
> ¼ cup honey
>
> ¼ cup rice wine vinegar
>
> 4 tablespoons fresh lime juice
>
> 4 tablespoons tamari

1. Measure everything into a blender or food processor.
2. Blend until very smooth.

The dressing keeps about one week when refrigerated.

Faux Cheese Sauce

Makes about 2 cups.

Once again we use the "jar method" to blend the tahini, flour, and water together. This recipe actually doesn't call for any vegan cheeses, since we devised it years ago before vegan cheeses were widely available. If you want a cheesier version, add about 1/4 cup grated vegan cheese. And yes, it works great as a sauce for macaroni, if you yearn for that kiddie mac and cheese experience.

Ingredients

½ cup water

2 tablespoons oat flour

2 tablespoons nutritional yeast

1 tablespoon mustard powder

½ teaspoon turmeric

2 tablespoons margarine

½ teaspoon garlic salt

½ cup soy milk

1 tablespoon tahini

1. Put flour, tahini and water in a jar. Cover, and shake vigorously until the tahini is dissolved.

2. Put the mixture in a small saucepan and heat on medium.

3. Stir in the remaining ingredients until mixture begins to bubble.

4. Turn heat to low and continue stirring until sauce thickens

Quick Ways With Bread

E ven though, we like to bake bread, in this cookbook we just focus on quick vegan breads and bread fixings. Our favorite quick bread is biscuits. Our hearty melt-in-your-mouth biscuits take only a few minutes to prepare.

When you're craving hot bread, but want to avoid those refrigerated horrors filled with trans fats and strange ingredients you can't pronounce, just whip up a batch of our Vegan Biscuits (page 26). We've included 10 different variations on them, and we urge you to try them all.

For those times when you want something a little more like traditional bread, there are two types of Vegan Soda Bread you can try (page 30). One is a savory loaf with garlic and herbs, the other is a plain, just slightly sweet version that goes with any meal.

We've also decided to share our version of foolproof bread machine pizza dough, plus three suggested pizza toppings. And finally, a few quick and clever vegan things you can do to jazz up store-bought or leftover bread, and our delicious recipe for pancakes or waffles.

Check out the chapter on Vegan Sandwiches for more delicious and easy ways to enjoy soul-satisfying bread every day.

Vegan Biscuits

Makes 12-15 biscuits (depending on size)

Can you really make biscuits without buttermilk or eggs? Yes! Just mix, knead, and roll out this dough gently. Try to work with as soft a dough as possible, since every addition of flour will make your biscuits a tiny bit heavier.

This dough is extremely forgiving. The cornmeal not only adds a nice, subtle, earthy flavor, but it gives the dough some "bite." Biscuits are the ultimate quick bread. They satisfy that fresh bread craving without all the fuss.

We haven't given an exact number of servings here because you can cut the biscuits into large triangles, like scones, or make smaller biscuits by using a cookie cutter. Very small biscuits take less time to bake; be sure to check them at around 9 minutes.

These biscuits are wonderful with just about any dish. Serve them for breakfast or brunch with Tofu Scramble (page 174) or sautéed veggies. Sweet biscuits can be delicious all by themselves with just a little margarine, preserves, fresh fruit, and café au lait.

For brunch, lunch, and parties, split savory biscuits open. Fill them with hummus or eggplant spread, chopped raw onion, chopped tomato, and some fresh chopped parsley. They make terrific finger sandwiches with baked tofu and/or shaved vegan cheese.

For dinner, you can serve biscuits with soups, stews, or salads. Split hot biscuits open, top with steamed cauliflower, and smother everything with Rich and Hearty Vegan Tomato Sauce (page 14). Or for a truly "ahhhh" moment, pour our heavenly Real Gravy (page 12) on fresh-from-the-oven biscuits. Mmmmm....

Ingredients

   2 cups unbleached flour

   2-½ teaspoons baking powder

   1 teaspoons salt

   ¼ cup cornmeal

   1-2 teaspoons dried herbs and spices (see the variations on the next page for a few suggestions)

   ⅓ cup oil

   ⅔ cup plain soy milk

   ½ teaspoon sugar

1. Preheat the oven to 425 degrees, and lightly oil a cookie sheet.

2. With a wire whisk, mix the flour, baking powder, salt, cornmeal, and spices together in a large mixing bowl until everything is distributed evenly.

3. Add the oil, and cut into the dry ingredients with a pastry cutter or long-tined fork until it starts to form balls about the size of a pea.

4. Add the milk very slowly, stirring until the dough is soft, but not sticky. Depending on how dry your flour is, you may need to stop before you add all the milk. Or you may need to add a tablespoon of water (or two) to achieve the correct consistency. Try not to add flour, but if you must, sprinkle it over the surface of the dough and work it in as gently possible, a tablespoon at a time.

5. Flour your hands, turn the dough out onto a floured surface, and knead it gently a few times. Then roll it out with a rolling pin until it is about ½ inch thick.

6. Cut the dough into biscuits using a knife or a cookie cutter. Bake 12-15 minutes on the oiled baking sheet.

10 Vegan Biscuit Variations

Here are 10 savory and sweet variations on the basic biscuit recipe that appears on the previous page.

Hot Cajun: Add 1 teaspoon commercial Cajun seasoning and ½ teaspoon dried red pepper flakes *or* ¼ teaspoon of cayenne pepper. Use a little less salt if the Cajun seasoning contains salt.

Italian: Add ½ teaspoon *each* of dried oregano, dried basil, and dried parsley. Dunk the biscuits in Rich and Hearty Vegan Tomato Sauce (page 14), or spread with hummus.

Pepper: If you love pepper, add ¼ teaspoon of black or mixed cracked pepper, or red pepper flakes. You could also add a pinch or two of sweet paprika. This variation is wonderful with creamy soups or mesclun salads.

Cheese Flavor: Add ½ cup shredded vegan cheese, or ¼ cup vegan parmesan when you stir in the soy milk. Serve for breakfast, with salads and soups, or split and fill with apple butter.

Greek: Add ½ teaspoon of dried thyme, ½ teaspoon of Greek Oregano, ¼ teaspoon of dried mint, and ½ teaspoon grated lemon peel. Wonderful with spinach salad. Or split the biscuits open, spread with a little tahini paste, and stuff with grilled eggplant and sliced Roma tomatoes.

Chocolate Chip: No, I'm not kidding. If you've never tried this, get ready for a treat. These biscuits are reminiscent of a good chocolate croissant, minus the dairy fat and hours of work! Just stir in ½ cup finely chopped dark chocolate or semi-sweet chips while adding the soy milk. These are best eaten straight out of the oven, with hot coffee.

Cinnamon: Add ½ -1 teaspoon of cinnamon and 2 teaspoon of raw sugar. Add 1 teaspoon of vanilla extract to the soy milk. You could also sprinkle a little cinnamon-sugar mixture on top of the biscuits before baking. Lovely for breakfast with café au lait.

Autumn Spice: Add 1-2 teaspoons of Pumpkin Pie Spice and a couple of tablespoons of raw sugar. Serve these biscuits with warm fruit (like baked or poached pears, baked or sautéed apples, or sautéed peaches), apple or pear butter, and hot cocoa.

Cranberry-Orange: Toss a handful of dried cranberries and about a teaspoon of grated orange zest into a small bowl. Add ⅓ cup of water or orange juice (if you have it), and microwave for about 20 seconds on High power, just until the cranberries plump up. Let this mixture cool while you measure everything else and cut in the oil. Add the fruit mixture with the soy milk, which you should reduce by ⅓ cup.

Honey Nut: This variation is another one that sounds odd, but is actually really good. Finely crush ½ cup of honey roasted peanuts, cashews, or pecans, and add to the dough with the soy milk. Serve hot, with warmed honey or maple syrup, or spread with peanut butter and jelly.

Vegan Herb And Garlic Soda Bread

1 standard size loaf.

This recipe is basically a soda bread with a couple of unique additions. It includes chopped garlic, rosemary and thyme, and a pinch of black pepper. It works with all kinds of dishes, but we like it best with creamy dishes, like the Creamy Potato Soup (page 144) or the Tempeh Stroganoff (page 166).

You don't have to understand anything about baking bread to successfully make soda bread. It's not much more complicated than making biscuits. You just have to knead the dough a bit before you shape it and bake it.

Ingredients

- 1 cup unbleached all purpose flour
- 1 cup whole wheat pastry flour
- 2 teaspoons baking soda
- 2 teaspoons baking powder
- 2 tablespoons sugar
- 2 cloves garlic, finely minced
- ¼ teaspoon dried rosemary, crushed (or 1 tablespoon fresh, chopped)
- ¼ teaspoon dried thyme (or 1 teaspoon fresh)
- ¼ cup vegan margarine
- 1-¼ cups plain soy milk

1. Preheat the oven to 375 degrees.

2. Combine the flours, baking soda and powder, and sugar in a large bowl.

3. Add the vegan margarine, cutting it in with a pastry blender, just as you would when making biscuits, until the dough is in pieces about the size of split peas.

4. Add the minced garlic and herbs to the soy milk, and stir well. Add the milk mixture to the dry ingredients, and mix until the dough just starts to hold together. You can add a tablespoon of soy milk or water if you need to, or sprinkle a little extra flour on the dough if it's very wet.

5. Scoop up the dough, turn it out on a board that's been dusted with a little bit of flour, and knead it lightly for a minute or two, no more.

6. Shape it into a rough loaf, set it into a bread pan that's been very lightly oiled, and bake for about 40 minutes. Don't try cutting it when it's hot. Let it cool for about 10 minutes before serving.

Simple Honey Wheat Vegan Quick Bread

1 standard size loaf.

This bread is like a classic Irish Soda bread, but mellowed with honey and made heartier with the addition of cracked wheat. It may remind you a little bit of those soft, miniature whole wheat loaves served in some restaurants; it's light, slightly sweet, and designed to satisfy the urge for hot bread.

You can serve this bread with just about anything. Although it is best when eaten the day it's made, it makes very good toast. Try using the leftovers in the Hot Garlic Slices recipe (page 38) and you won't be disappointed.

Ingredients

1 cup unbleached all purpose flour

1 cup whole wheat pastry flour

¼ cup cracked wheat

2 teaspoons baking soda

2 teaspoons baking powder

4 tablespoons vegan margarine

1 cup plain soy milk (approximately)

¼ cup honey

1. Preheat the oven to 375 degrees.

2. Combine the flours, cracked wheat, baking soda and powder in a large bowl.

3. Add the vegan margarine, cutting it in with a pastry blender, just as you would when making biscuits, until the dough is in pieces about the size of split peas.

4. Add the honey to the soy milk, microwave for about 20 seconds until warm, and stir well.

5. Add the milk mixture to the dry ingredients, and mix until the dough just starts to hold together. You can add a tablespoon of soy milk or water if you need to, or sprinkle a little extra flour on the dough if it's very wet.

6. Scoop up the dough, turn it out on a board that's been dusted with a little bit of flour, and knead it lightly for a minute or two, no more.

7. Shape it into a rough loaf, set it into a bread pan that's been very lightly oiled, and bake for about 40 minutes. Don't cut when it's hot – let it cool for about 10 minutes before serving.

Bread Machine Pizza Dough

Dough for a 12-inch pizza.

This is our all time favorite, easy, foolproof dough for pizza, calzones, and even pierogies (if you're feeling ambitious).

We have a Zojirushi bread machine, but we never use it to actually bake the bread. We use it to make dough and then bake the dough in the oven. This recipe should work in any machine that makes 1.5-pound loaves and has a "dough" setting.

The crushed red pepper is optional. You can omit it, or substitute dried oregano, basil, or Italian seasoning. For some reason, the red pepper isn't really hot by the time the dough is done, so don't worry about the heat. Plus, it adds a nice aroma to the dough.

Ingredients

- 1-⅛ cups water
- 1 tablespoon olive oil
- 1 tablespoon sugar
- 1 teaspoon salt
- 2 teaspoons red pepper flakes (or dried spices of your choosing)
- 1 cup whole wheat flour
- 2 cups bread flour
- 1-¼ teaspoons yeast

1. Put all the ingredients into the bread machine, and start the dough cycle.

2. When the machine is done, shape the dough into the desired shape (pizza, calzone or whatever). Add toppings, or fill and bake for 30 minutes at 400 degrees.

Three Nice Pizza Toppings

The vegan cheese in these recipes is optional. You can still make a wonderful pizza by omitting the cheese and adding more veggies. To make the pizza taste as rich and satisfying as dairy pizza, melt a tablespoon or two of vegan margarine, and drizzle over the pizza after it comes out of the oven.

Traditional:

1 cup Hearty Vegan Tomato Sauce (page 14)

1 cup shredded vegan mozzarella cheese

1 roma tomato, sliced very thin

1 clove garlic, minced fine

1-2 teaspoons dried Italian seasoning, or 2 tablespoons chopped fresh basil

Sprinkling of crushed red pepper flakes

Mushroom and Onion:

1 cup Hearty Vegan Tomato Sauce (page 14)

1 cup shredded vegan mozzarella cheese

1 cup sliced, sautéed mushrooms

½ cup chopped red onion

1 clove garlic, minced fine

1 teaspoon dried oregano

Three Nice Pizza Toppings (continued)

Supreme:

1 cup Hearty Vegan Tomato Sauce (page 14)

1 cup shredded vegan mozzarella cheese

1 cup fresh spinach, chopped fine

1 roma tomato, sliced very thin

1 small green or red pepper, chopped

¼ cup sliced pitted black olives

1 cup sliced, sautéed mushrooms

½ cup chopped red onion

1 thick slice Slow Roasted Tofu (page 170), crumbled (optional)

2 cloves garlic, sliced thin

1 teaspoon dried oregano

1 teaspoon crushed red pepper flakes

Torta Rustica

You can use your Bread Machine Pizza Dough to make things other than pizza, such as calzones, pirogues, or this easy Torta Rustica. Instead of rolling out one round as you would for pizza, you roll out two: one for the bottom crust and one for the top. The filling is great for pirogues or calzones too. One batch of pizza dough makes 32 pirogues or four big calzones. If you have time, we can report that pirogues go over **big** at potlucks. Even non-vegetarians love them.

Ingredients

- 1 batch of Bread Machine Pizza Dough (page 34)
- 1 box frozen spinach
- 1 tomato, chopped
- 3 cups mixed frozen vegetables
- 1 silken tofu
- 3 tablespoons vegan sour cream
- 3 tablespoons nutritional yeast
- 1 teaspoon garlic salt
- 1 teaspoon basil

1. Preheat oven to 375 degrees. Defrost and drain frozen vegetables.

2. Mash tofu in a medium bowl. Mix in defrosted vegetables with tofu, sour cream, tomato, nutritional yeast, garlic salt and basil.

3. Cut dough into two pieces. Divide it so one piece uses about ⅔ the dough for the bottom crust and one uses ⅓ of the dough for the top. Roll out bottom crust and place in 2-quart casserole dish.

4. Put vegetable mixture in casserole

5. Roll out the top crust and lay on top. Seal the edges by pinching with your fingers and/or crimping with a fork.

6. Cut a few ½ inch long holes in the top so steam can escape. Bake for 30 minutes until the crust is golden brown.

Hot Garlic Slices

Serves 2.

This recipe is an easy vegan variation on garlic bread, and delicious when served with any kind of salad, soup, or pasta. It's also great with Blender Hummus (page 134) or Curried Eggless Egg Salad (page 133).

At the height of tomato season, try this decadent treat. It may sound weird, but it's delicious. Slice a couple of big, juicy vine-ripened tomatoes. Sprinkle them with a tiny bit of salt and a generous grinding of black pepper, and refrigerate. Make Hot Garlic Slices, and add about 2 teaspoons of honey to the spread. Pull the bread out of the oven, top with the tomatoes, and eat.

Ingredients

4 1-inch thick slices of leftover Simple Honey Wheat Vegan Quick Bread (page 32)

1 clove garlic, minced very fine

2 tablespoons vegan margarine

2 tablespoons extra virgin olive oil

Pinch dried oregano, basil, or crushed red pepper flakes (optional)

1. Preheat a toaster oven to 350 degrees.
2. Mix the garlic, margarine, olive oil, and optional herbs until thoroughly mixed.
3. Spread each slice of bread with a tablespoon of the margarine mixture.
4. Place directly on the wire rack in the toaster oven, and bake until hot but not dry (about 3 minutes).

Savory Pitas

4 pitas.

These pitas only take a minute or two to prepare, and they make a simple meal of hummus and vegetable stew into a special treat.

The idea is to create moist, hot pitas with a slightly buttery taste, not to crisp them. If you are unfortunate enough to be stuck with stale, dry, store-bought pitas, this technique is a good way to soften them and punch up their flavor.

Ingredients

4 pita breads (preferably whole wheat or sprouted grain)

2 tablespoons vegan margarine

1 teaspoon dried herbs of your choice (try basil, thyme, or ¼ teaspoon crushed mint)

1. Preheat the toaster oven or conventional oven to 375 degrees.
2. Melt the vegan margarine with the herbs in a small bowl in the microwave.
3. Take a sheet of aluminum foil, and lay a pita on it. Sprinkle it with a few scant drops of water, then brush with the melted margarine. Lay another pita on top of it, sprinkle, and brush. Fold the foil over until both pitas are loosely wrapped. Make a second packet with the other two pitas.
4. Bake for about 10 minutes, turning the packets over once. Serve the pitas right from the foil so they are nice and hot.
5. You could also make these pitas on an outdoor grill, cooking over the coals for about 10-15 minutes, depending on how hot the fire is.

Double-Corn Cornbread

One 8 x 8 pan (about 16 squares)

It has taken years for us to find a cornbread recipe we like. Most cornbread is dry, tasteless, or both. This recipe actually goes together quite easily and can include a number of optional ingredients, depending on your taste. The main thing is that it isn't dry as dirt. The recipe calls for creamed corn, but if you don't have it around, you can use defrosted frozen corn and increase the milk by about ⅛ cup.

Ingredients

1 cup cream style corn

1 cup soymilk

2 teaspoons apple cider vinegar

½ cup vegan "cheddar" cheese (optional)

4 green onions (optional)

2 jalapeno peppers, seeded, cored and chopped (optional)

¼ cup oil

1 "egg" (1-½ teaspoons egg replacer mixed with 2 tablespoons of water)

1 cup cornmeal

1 cup flour

2 tablespoons light brown sugar

2 teaspoons baking powder

½ teaspoon salt

1. Preheat oven to 375 degrees. Spray an 8 x 8 pan with spray canola oil.

2. In a small bowl, combine soymilk and vinegar. Let stand 5 minutes.

3. Add corn, cheese, jalapenos, onions, oil, and the "egg" to the soymilk mixture. Set aside.

4. In a medium bowl, combine cornmeal, flour, sugar, baking powder, and salt.

5. Add the soymilk mixture into the flour mixture and stir to mix thoroughly.

6. Put in greased pan and bake for 35 minutes. Let cool for 10 minutes before slicing.

Perfect Vegan Pancake or Waffle Mix

4 large waffles, or about 8 4-inch pancakes.

People often say you can't make light, fluffy, tender pancakes or waffles without eggs or buttermilk. Nonsense! The secret is to measure carefully. If you use a little too much flour, your pancakes will be heavy. You should also mix the ingredients with as few strokes as possible so you don't activate the gluten in the flour.

Using this recipe, you get anywhere from four big waffles to a dozen tiny pancakes. Serve your pancakes or waffles with all the good stuff: vegan margarine, pure maple syrup, honey, or preserves.

Ingredients

1 cup buckwheat, oat, or whole wheat flour

¾ cup whole wheat pastry flour

¾ teaspoon baking soda

1 tablespoon egg replacer

2 tablespoons sweetener (honey, syrup, molasses, or sugar)

⅓ cup sunflower oil

1-⅔ cups soy milk

¼ cup chopped nuts (optional)

1. Preheat your waffle iron or pan.
2. Combine dry ingredients in medium mixing bowl.
3. Combine liquid ingredients in large mixing bowl.
4. Combine dry ingredients with liquid ingredients and mix.
5. Pour batter into pan or waffle iron and cook.

Potatoes, Pastas, Rice, Stuffing

L et's face it, vegans eat a lot of carbohydrates. During the days of high-protein diets, carbs became unfashionable, but many vegans have no trouble controlling their weight, even though they eat bread, pasta, potatoes, or rice at almost every meal.

Realistically, vegans can control their intake of fats without much effort. When you're not eating meat or cheese, the number of fat calories you're consuming is drastically reduced.

The fats most vegans eat tend to be high quality and easily digestible, like olive oil and avocados. You can even buy vegan margarines that don't contain all the nasty, hydrogenated trans fats that are the real culprit behind many diseases.

Vegans do eat plenty of easily absorbed proteins, like beans and tofu, that are also heart healthy. When we switched to a plant-based diet, we were rewarded with more energy and weight loss.

Everyone is different, so like the old saying goes, your mileage may vary. But one thing's for sure, good quality carbs are essential to feeling full and happy when you're eating vegan. You really count on those delicious pastas, pilafs, and potatoes to ease your hunger pangs. When you're craving some good old fashioned comfort food, nothing beats mashed potatoes or stuffing alongside your veggies.

Here are our favorite dishes that feature pasta, rice, and potatoes. As a special treat, we're sharing our easy stuffing recipe. This one always goes fast; even non-vegans love it.

Mustard Roasted Potatoes With Herbs

4 generous side-dish portions, or 2 main dish portions with steamed or baked vegetables.

This dish is for mustard fans. If you are tired of overly rich or overly bland potato dishes, this one will make you smile. It works in so many contexts, from brunch to lunch to holiday suppers. It's a nice change from the standard garlic-rosemary potatoes.

You can offer these potatoes as finger food by sticking a toothpick in each chunk. (Yes, it's two minutes worth of extra work, but hey it's a party!)

The refined flavor of Dijon mustard combined with earthy potatoes compliments a wide variety of non-starchy vegetable combinations. It's especially appealing with tangy sweet tomato-based dishes, or with mild curries.

For a simple cold-weather supper, assemble this dish, pop it into the oven, then curl up in front of the fire, and read for half an hour. Then throw together a spinach salad, preferably with a Creamy Italian Dressing (page 19) or Mild Sesame-Peanut Dressing (page 23), and you've definitely got yourself a meal.

Ingredients

⅓ cup Dijon mustard

2 tablespoons olive oil

1 clove garlic, chopped

½ teaspoon dried Italian seasoning, or 1 tablespoon fresh thyme

2 pounds medium red-skinned potatoes, cut into chunks

1. Preheat the oven to 425 degrees.

2. Stir all the ingredients, except the potatoes, together in a small bowl.

3. Place the potatoes in a lightly greased 13 x 9 x 2 inch baking pan, or on a shallow baking sheet.

4. Drizzle the mustard mixture over the potatoes, toss them around to coat them with the mustard dressing, then spread them in a single layer.

5. Bake at 425 degrees, stirring occasionally, for 35 to 40 minutes, or until the potatoes are tender when pierced with a fork.

Five Different Mustard Roasted Potatoes With Herbs

All of these variations on the basic Mustard Roasted Potatoes have a distinctive twist. We have suggested a few menus they would compliment, but feel free to create your own "fusion" menus and serve them with whatever you like.

Spicy Mustard Potatoes

Substitute hot mustard for the Dijon mustard. Start with a couple of tablespoons, and taste the sauce before adding it to the pan, so you don't overdo it. For the herbs, substitute ½ teaspoon cumin, and ½ teaspoon chili powder. Add a couple of sliced cloves of garlic to the potatoes before baking. Serve the spuds with Middle Eastern dishes, such as Baba Eggplant (page 100).

Honey Mustard Onion Potatoes

Increase the olive oil a tiny bit, and add a large Vidalia onion or two, cut into smallish chunks. Substitute 2-3 tablespoons of honey mustard for the Dijon, and add a sprinkling of paprika before popping the pan into the oven. This variation is good with any mildly flavored protein dish, such as Chicken Fried Tofu Cutlets (page 158) or Slow Roasted Tofu (page 170).

Dijon Mustard Sweet Potatoes

If you like sweet potatoes, try them in this recipe. It's a nice change from the ubiquitous honey or maple syrup sweet potatoes, yet just as delicious. Substitute sweet potatoes cut into 1 inch cubes for the regular potatoes, and ½ teaspoon of nutmeg or dried ginger for the Italian Seasoning.

Creole Mustard Potatoes

This variation is the perfect hot and spicy accompaniment to Chicken Fried Tofu Cutlets (page 158). Substitute 3-4 tablespoons Creole Mustard for the Dijon, and add 2 or 3 seeded and chopped jalapeno peppers, then bake as directed.

Horseradish Mustard Potatoes

Substitute 2-3 tablespoons Horseradish Mustard for the Dijon, and add 1 tablespoon vegan bacon bits, and a small chopped red onion before baking.

Potato Salad with Mixed Olives

Serves 6.

This warm potato salad recipe features the unusual combination of potatoes and olives. You could add more exotic olives, such as kalamatas, but make sure you pit, drain, and rinse them well.

This salad keeps very well for several days. Warm it in the microwave before serving it with some simple steamed spinach.

Ingredients

3 tablespoons olive oil

¼ cup rice vinegar or white wine vinegar (plus extra for sprinkling)

3 tablespoons minced shallots

1 teaspoon Dijon mustard

2 teaspoons fresh flat leaf parsley, chopped

3 tablespoons fresh basil, chopped

2 pounds Yukon Gold potatoes, peeled and cut into ½ inch chunks

½ cup red onion, chopped

½ cup green olives halved

½ cup black olives halved

¼ cup capers, drained

Salt and freshly ground black pepper to taste

1. Steam the potatoes in a steamer basket about 12 minutes, or until they are tender when pierced with a fork.

2. Mix the olive oil, vinegar, mustard, and shallots in a small bowl, then whisk in the parsley and basil. Whisk in salt and pepper to taste, then in the microwave for about 30 seconds.

3. Drain the potatoes, and place in a large serving bowl. Sprinkle them with a little vinegar.

4. Pour the dressing over the potatoes, and toss together.

5. Add the onion, the black and green olives, and the capers, and toss again.

6. Serve warm or at room temperature.

Potatoes Roasted with Carrots, Onions, Rosemary and Sage

Serves 4-6.

This recipe is similar to standard rosemary potatoes, but it is more tender, slightly crisp, and much more interesting with the addition of onions and carrots.

You can vary the proportions of the vegetables as much as you wish. In fact, I once made this dish with just a couple of pounds of carrots, and it was incredible.

This dish is perfect with any kind of green vegetables. For a big dinner party, serve it with Slow Roasted Tofu (page 170) and a green bean dish or broccoli topped with Vegan Hollandaise (page 16).

Ingredients

  3 tablespoons vegetable broth mix

  2 tablespoons olive oil

  2 cloves garlic, minced

  2 tablespoons minced fresh rosemary, or 1 teaspoon dried

  1 tablespoon minced fresh sage leaves or ½ teaspoon dried

  1¼ pounds potatoes, scrubbed and cut into small chunks

  2 medium onions, cut into small chunks

  3 carrots, chopped

  ¼ teaspoon salt

  Freshly ground black pepper to taste

1. Preheat the oven to 425 degrees.

2. Spray a 13 x 9 inch baking dish with with nonstick canola oil cooking spray.

3. In a large bowl, whisk together the broth, oil, garlic, rosemary, sage, salt, and pepper.

4. Add the potatoes, onions, and carrots, and toss well.

5. Spread the vegetables evenly in the baking dish. Cover tightly with aluminum foil.

6. Roast for 20 minutes, until just slightly tender.

7. Remove the foil, stir and roast for up to 30 minutes more until crisp and golden.

Vegan Stuffed Potatoes

12 stuffed potato halves.

These potatoes can be a meal in themselves or a spectacular side dish for a holiday meal.

Ingredients

    6 baking potatoes

    1 10-ounce package fresh baby spinach leaves, chopped

    ¼ cup plain full fat soy milk

    ½ cup vegan cream cheese

    1 tablespoon dried parsley

    1 teaspoon dried thyme

    ½ teaspoon garlic powder

    1 chopped roma tomato

    Sweet paprika

1. Wash the potatos and pierce them with a fork. Bake them for 55 minutes at 400 degrees. Allow them to cool about 10 minutes, then cut them in half lengthwise and scoop out most of the innards and place them into a large mixing bowl.

2. Add the soy milk, vegan cream cheese, herbs and spices into the bowl. Thoroughly whip the mixture, using a hand beater or an electric mixer on medium low speed. Taste, and add salt and pepper. Stir in the baby spinach and scoop the mixture back into the potato skins.

3. Place the filled potatoes on a greased cookie sheet.

4. Sprinkle each potato half with a little paprika and bake in a 400 degree oven for 15 minutes.

5. Top with the chopped tomato and serve hot.

Vegan Mashed Potatoes

Serve 6-8.

These potatoes could be called "smashed potatoes" because they are better if you mash them by hand (plus using a potato masher can be cathartic after a long day at work). Adding vegan sour cream or mayonnaise contributes to a creamy, rich-tasting mashed potato. The chopped fresh chives are a nice touch, especially if you have decided not to serve Real Gravy (page 12) on top. You can add other good things to mashed potatoes, like minced garlic, fresh or dried herbs, sautéed onions, and peppers.

Ingredients

2 pounds (about 6 medium) potatoes, peeled and cut into small chunks

¼ - ½ cup plain soy milk

2 tablespoons vegan margarine

3 tablespoons vegan sour cream or 1 tablespoon vegan mayonnaise

2 tablespoons fresh chives, minced (optional)

1. Boil about 3 quarts of salted water over high heat.

2. Add the potatoes, and reduce the heat to a simmer. Cook uncovered about 25-30 minutes, or until the potatoes are soft but not falling apart.

3. When they are done, drain the potatoes well, and put them back in the pot along with the margarine.

4. Mash the potatoes using a hand potato masher. Pour in the milk a little at a time.

5. Fold in the vegan sour cream or mayonnaise and chopped chives, and serve immediately.

Spicy Potato Salad with Dill

Serve 4-6.

You can make this fragrant, slightly spicy potato dish with tiny new potatoes. Just make sure you scrub them really well, and then cut them in half. This recipe is a variation on the classic hot potato salad. You can actually serve this dish hot, at room temperature, or chilled.

Serve with plenty of steamed or lightly sautéed fresh spinach.

Ingredients

2 pounds red-skinned potatoes, cut into 2 inch chunks

1 red bell pepper, chopped

1 small onion, chopped

4 tablespoons vegan mayonnaise

6 tablespoons plain soy yogurt

¼ cup fresh dill, chopped

1 tablespoon Dijon mustard

1 tablespoon balsamic vinegar

1 tablespoon prepared white horseradish

1. Cook the potatoes in a pot of boiling salted water until just tender, about 15-20 minutes. Drain.

2. Combine the potatoes, pepper and onion in a large bowl.

3. Whisk together the vegan mayonnaise, soy yogurt, dill, mustard, vinegar, and horseradish. If serving hot, pour all the dressing over the warm potatoes, toss, and pop into the microwave for about 30 seconds to kick up the temperature.

4. If serving cold, add only about half the dressing to the potatoes, and toss. Refrigerate 1 hour to overnight, and refrigerate the remaining dressing. Right before serving, add the rest of the dressing and mix well.

Rotini with Black Beans and Tomatoes

Serves 4.

This dish has the Cuban flavors of lime, cilantro, and cumin. If you wish, you can omit the cumin, substitute lemon zest for the lime, and use chopped fresh basil instead of cilantro. The Tabasco is optional of course. If you like the distinctive heat and aroma of Tabasco, go ahead and add more.

The microwave method only warms up this chunky sauce. The tomatoes shouldn't really be cooked, just warmed up a bit. This dish is a great one to make in summer with vine-ripened tomatoes. You could also make it with a pound of cherry tomatoes cut in half.

Ingredients

¼ cup olive oil

1 large garlic clove, finely chopped

1 15-ounce can black beans, drained and rinsed

1 pound fresh ripe tomatoes, diced

Zest of 1 large lime, finely grated

1 teaspoon Tabasco sauce (optional)

1 teaspoon dried oregano

1 teaspoon ground cumin

½ teaspoon salt

¼ cup fresh cilantro leaves, chopped

½ pound tricolor rotini pasta

1. Combine all the ingredients except the pasta and fresh cilantro in a microwave-safe serving bowl.

2. Cook the pasta, drain, and rinse with hot water.

3. Microwave the bean mixture for about 1 minute on high power, just long enough to warm it up.

4. Add the drained hot pasta to the bowl, toss, and sprinkle with cilantro.

Pasta with Spicy Sesame Vegetables

Serves 4.

This recipe is extremely adaptable. If you don't have fresh broccoli, cauliflower, or snap peas, check your freezer for frozen veggies. Tofu is another nice addition if you are looking for some protein in your dinner. The main goal is to end up with about three cups of veggie "stuff" to put on top of the pasta.

Ingredients

3 cups ziti or other tube-type pasta

2 teaspoons dark sesame oil

1 tablespoon peanut oil

3 cloves garlic, finely chopped

1 tablespoon chopped fresh ginger

½ cup water

1 cup broccoli florets

1 cup cauliflower florets

1 cup sugar snap peas

1 block of firm tofu (optional)

¼ cup tamari

¼ cup water

2 tablespoons tahini paste

2 teaspoons arrowroot

2 teaspoons crushed dried red pepper flakes (or more if desired)

1. Put a large pot of water on to boil.

2. In a large skillet over medium heat, warm up the two oils. Add the garlic and ginger, and cook gently so the garlic does not burn (about 1-2 minutes).

3. Add the vegetables and the ½ cup water to the skillet. Reduce the heat to simmering temperature. Cover and cook until the vegetables are barely tender but not soft, about 8 minutes.

4. Add the pasta to the pot of boiling water.

5. Put tahini, tamari, water, and arrowroot into a jar. Cover, and shake to dissolve the tahini.

6. Uncover the vegetables, turn up the heat to medium, and add the tamari and tahini paste mixture. Simmer until the sauce thickens slightly, about 5 minutes, stirring occasionally.

7. When the pasta is ready, drain quickly and put back into the pot or into a serving bowl.

8. Add the hot vegetable mixture, toss, and serve.

Pasta with Garlic and White Beans

Serves 2-4.

This dish is for garlic lovers. You could reduce the garlic, of course, but it's so delicious when combined with the creaminess of white beans and really good olive oil.

This recipe makes a nice late night meal because it's easy to throw together and can be made with things we all have on hand, such as canned beans, garlic, olive oil, and a few herbs. Chopping the garlic is the most work. If you don't feel like mincing it, slice it and just cook it a little longer so it mellows out.

A green salad is all you need to make this a complete meal. Try a little sprinkle of the vegan bacon bits, if you have them. They add a nice smoky scent and a little extra bite.

Ingredients

½ pound thin spaghetti (not angel hair) or linguine pasta

6 tablespoons extra virgin olive oil

3 tablespoons chopped flat leaf parsley (or 1 tablespoon dried)

½ teaspoon sea salt

¼ teaspoon freshly ground black pepper

6 cloves garlic, minced

1 teaspoon dried basil

1 teaspoon crushed red pepper flakes

1 15-ounce can Great Northern or Canellini beans, drained and rinsed well

Vegan bacon bits (optional)

1 fresh tomato, chopped (optional)

1. Bring a large pot of water to a boil and add the pasta.

2. Meanwhile, heat the olive oil over medium heat. Add the parsley, sea salt, pepper, garlic, basil, and red pepper flakes. Reduce the heat and cook for about 2 minutes. Make sure the garlic does not brown.

3. Add the beans and gently heat through.

4. Drain the pasta, and place it into a serving bowl. Add the garlic bean mixture to the bowl and mix together well. If you wish, add a sprinkling of vegan bacon bits and the tomato, and mix some more.

5. Serve immediately.

Pasta with Artichokes and Olives

Serves 2.

This dish works almost any time. You can make it for brunch, lunch, dinner, or as a late night snack, after you've come home from a night on the town. The sauce can be ready in the time it takes to cook the pasta. It's easy to assemble from things most of us have on hand, like tomato, peppers, onion, garlic, and canned artichokes.

If you don't have fresh bell peppers, try adding half a jar of drained pimentos, or chop a few roasted red peppers packed in olive oil. If you love garlic, you can add another clove if you wish. Nothing complements artichokes like fresh garlic. But be judicious. The beauty of this dish is the way the artichokes dominate; they taste tart, sunny, and lively.

Ingredients

¼ pound spaghetti or linguini, roughly broken into halves or thirds

1 14-ounce can artichoke hearts packed in water, rinsed, and drained

2 sweet peppers (red or green or mixed), chopped

⅓ cup onion, finely chopped

2 cloves garlic, finely chopped

1 tablespoon olive oil

1 medium fresh tomato, chopped

¼ cup fresh chopped basil (or 2 teaspoons dried)

2 tablespoons grated vegan cheese (optional)

1. Cook pasta in plenty of boiling salted water according to package directions.

2. While the pasta cooks, heat the olive oil in a large skillet until it's hot, but not smoking.

3. Stir the rinsed artichokes, peppers, onions, and garlic into the olive oil. Watch the heat. Keep stirring so the garlic doesn't burn. Reduce the heat to medium-high and cook, stirring constantly, until tender (about 5 minutes, depending on how soft you like your onions).

4. Stir in the chopped tomato and basil. Cook about 2 minutes, or until heated through.

5. Drain the pasta and empty it into a large bowl. Add the sauce, toss gently to mix.

6. To serve, pile the pasta into warmed bowls or plates, and sprinkle with a little vegan cheese or hot red pepper flakes. Serve with generous helpings of a salad of mixed greens, tossed with freshly cracked pepper, a little lemon juice, and olive oil.

Broccoli Couscous with Marinated Tomatoes

Serves 2.

Couscous is one of life's easy foods, since it basically cooks itself. If you can boil water, you can make couscous. By just adding a few spices and some veggies, you can turn plain couscous into a tasty meal in about 20 minutes.

Ingredients

1 onion, chopped

2 broccoli stalks, chopped

1 box couscous

2 tablespoons olive oil

1 teaspoon flax seed

½ teaspoon crushed red pepper

¼ teaspoon celery seed

¼ teaspoon garlic granules

¼ cup water

1 bouillon cube

1 tomato chopped

½ teaspoon garlic salt

¼ teaspoon black pepper

¼ teaspoon dill weed

2-¼ cups water

1. Add the 2 tablespoons of olive oil to a large saucepan and add onion. Cook onions at medium heat until translucent.

2. Add flax seed, crushed red pepper, celery seed, garlic granules, broccoli, and ¼ cup water. Cover and steam until broccoli is bright green and tender, about 5 minutes.

3. While the broccoli is steaming, mix tomato, garlic salt, black pepper, and dill weed in small glass bowl. Let stand to marinate.

4. Remove the lid from the broccoli and add the 2-¼ cups of water and the bouillon cube. Heat until the mixture begins to bubble, stirring occasionally.

5. Stir in couscous, cover and remove from heat.

6. Let stand 10 minutes. Serve with marinated tomatoes spooned over the top.

Pasta Carbonara

Serves 4.

This carbonara has taste sensations reminiscent of the real thing, but without the eggs or bacon. We use vegan pepperoni for the "meaty" element. You might also experiment with the vegan Canadian bacon if you prefer its spicing. Using the packaged pepperoni is a lot easier than working with real bacon, so another benefit to this vegan carbonara is that it's certainly a lot easier to make than the real thing!

Ingredients

1 package spaghetti

2 tablespoons olive oil

1 package vegan pepperoni, chopped

1 onion, chopped

½ cup fresh parsley or 3 tablespoons dried

1 silken aseptic tofu

¼ cup nutritional yeast

2 "eggs" (3 teaspoons egg replacer mixed with 4 tablespoons water)

1 cup soymilk

Red pepper flakes

1. Put water on to boil for pasta. Cook pasta according to package directions.

2. Put olive oil and onions in pan and cook onions until they are tender.

3. When the onions are cooked, remove from heat and set aside.

4. Take ¼ of the cooked onions from the pan and place in a blender or food processor. Add tofu, nutritional yeast, eggs, red pepper flakes, and soymilk. Blend thoroughly until creamy.

5. Chop the parsley and pepperoni and grate the cheese.

6. Put the pepperoni in the pan with the reserved onions. Cook briefly just to warm up the pepperoni.

7. When the spaghetti is done, drain. Return the pasta to the pot and mix in the sauce, pepperoni/onion mixture, parsley, and cheese. Serve immediately.

Middle Eastern Rice Pilaf

Serves 4.

This aromatic pilaf is filled with Middle Eastern spices like thyme, cinnamon, and allspice. The pilaf works well with virtually all the vegetable dishes in this book. It would also be the perfect accompaniment to Greek Tofu (page 171) or Brown Lentils With Sun-Dried Tomato Vinaigrette (page 168).

Ingredients

1 cup white basmatic or jasmine rice (preferably organic)

2 tablespoons olive oil

2 cloves garlic, minced

1 teaspoon dried thyme

½ teaspoon cinnamon

½ teaspoon allspice

½ teaspoon salt

3 tablespoons golden raisins or dried currants (optional)

2 cups hot vegetable stock (or use 1 Morga cube dissolved in boiling water)

1 cup fresh spinach, sliced in thin slivers or one 10-ounce package chopped spinach, defrosted and drained

1 cup frozen peas

1. Heat the oil in a large nonstick skillet over medium-high heat. Add the rice, garlic, thyme, cinnamon, allspice, salt, and raisins or currants. Stir everything around until the rice is coated with the oil and begins to take on just a little golden color.

2. Add the hot stock. Stir, bring to a boil, then reduce the heat to a low simmer, and cover the pan.

3. After about 10 minutes, check the pilaf. Most of the water should be absorbed, but it should still look a little wet. If there's still plenty of liquid, cover and cook another 5-10 minutes.

4. Once the water is almost completely absorbed, add the spinach and frozen peas. Cook uncovered for a few minutes until the peas are hot.

Asian Rice Pilaf

Serves 4.

This recipe has a lot of ingredients, but it's not difficult. Although the recipe uses much less oil than fried rice, it is just as flavorful. Serve it with Spinach Seasoned with Soy, Sesame, and Garlic (page 106).

Ingredients

  1 cup white jasmine rice

  1 tablespoon peanut oil

  1 clove garlic, minced

  1 tablespoon fresh ginger, grated (or 1 tablespoon grated ginger in a jar)

  ¼ teaspoon crushed red pepper flakes

  ½ cup carrots, diced fine

  2 tablespoons red bell pepper, seeded and chopped

  2 cups hot vegetable stock (use a Morga cube)

  2 tablespoons tamari

  1 teaspoon dark sesame oil

  ¼ cup unsalted cashews, chopped

  ¼ cup scallions, chopped

1. Heat the oil in a large nonstick skillet over medium-high heat. Add the rice, garlic, ginger, pepper flakes, carrots, and bell pepper, and stir everything around until the rice is coated with the oil and begins to take on just a little golden color.

2. Pour in the hot stock, tamari, and sesame oil. Bring to a boil, then reduce the heat to a low simmer, and cover the pan.

3. After about 10 minutes, check the pilaf. Most of the water should be absorbed, but it should still look a little wet. If there's still plenty of liquid, cover and cook another 5-10 minutes.

4. Once the water is almost completely absorbed, add the chopped cashews and scallions, and cook uncovered for a few more minutes.

Quick Vegan Stuffing

Serves 2-4.

This stuffing is moist, flavorful, and easy. You can use almost any type of bread except French or Italian. We like to use a good whole grain bread, but you can experiment or even use a combination.

For a more veggie-intensive stuffing, you may want to add a half a bag of frozen mixed veggies. Just defrost them in the microwave, drain, and throw them in with the peppers and the celery.

This dish is a natural for the holidays or a dinner party. You might serve it with Chicken Fried Tofu Cutlets (page 158) or Slow Roasted Tofu (page 170). And of course, don't forget the Real Gravy (page 12).

Ingredients

⅓ loaf of good quality bread

1 cup water

1 Morga bouillon cube

½ teaspoon sage

½ teaspoon crushed rosemary

½ teaspoon marjoram

½ red bell pepper, seeded and chopped

½ green bell pepper, seeded and chopped

½ large onion, chopped

½ teaspoon black pepper

½ teaspoon salt

2 tablespoons olive oil

¼ teaspoon crushed red pepper flakes

2 stalks celery, chopped

2 carrots, chopped or grated

½ bag frozen mixed vegetables (optional)

1. Slice bread into ½-inch slices and toast. Leave it in the toaster oven (with the oven off) to dry out.

2. Heat the water, bouillon, and spices in a sauce pan. Cover and simmer on low.

3. Chop up the vegetables. Defrost the frozen veggies, if using.

4. Heat the olive oil in a Dutch oven, and add the onion, carrots, and celery.

5. Chop the bread into ½-inch cubes.

6. When the onions are translucent, add the bread, peppers, and defrosted veggies (if using). Mix well.

7. Add the stock to the bread and vegetables, and mix thoroughly

8. Cover and cook on very low heat for about 15 minutes, stirring occasionally.

Mustard Grilled Vegetables with Pasta

Serves 4.

This recipe is easy to make and very flexible. You could use just zucchini and onions, onions and bell pepper, just mushrooms, or any other combination.

Ingredients

6 tablespoons Dijon mustard, divided

4 cups sliced vegetables cut in bite-sized pieces (try zucchini, crookneck squash, carrots, onions, mushrooms, and red bell pepper)

4 tablespoons extra virgin olive oil

1 clove garlic, minced

2 tablespoons fresh basil, chopped (or 1 teaspoon dried)

8 ounces penne pasta

1. Preheat the broiler or an outdoor grill. Put a pot of salted water on to boil. Add the pasta after the water comes to a rolling boil.

2. Brush 4 tablespoons of mustard on the vegetables, place them on a cookie sheet, and broil or grill until tender. Set them aside.

3. When the pasta is ready, drain, and place it into a serving bowl.

4. Add the vegetables to the pasta, and toss. Whisk the remaining mustard, oil, and basil together, and toss again. Serve hot, or at room temperature.

Vegetable-Centered Dishes

Vegans quickly learn to blur the traditional recipe categories. They find themselves treating side dishes as main dishes (since side dishes may be the only viable foods at a party or restaurant). Vegans end up eating their salad side by side with the potatoes or rice or have two different kinds of soup for dinner!

In this chapter, we have included all our favorite recipes in which vegetables (raw or cooked) predominate. The only exception is potatoes. You'll find spuds in the Pasta, Potatoes, and Rice chapter.

In the recipes that follow, we explain how the typical vegan might combine the dish with other vegetable or starch dishes to make a nice, satisfying meal. In some cases, a recipe can even be served hot, at room temperature, or cold.

One thing that all of these recipes have in common, however, is their ease of preparation. You don't have to master any gourmet cooking techniques to make these dishes successfully.

All of the recipes are very forgiving. If you overcook the vegetables a little bit, or slightly singe something, the overall dish won't really suffer. Unless you burn something to a crisp, the flavors will still be there!

Asparagus with Lemon Caper Vinaigrette

Serves 2 as a light lunch or first course.

This is a great dish to make in the spring, when fresh asparagus begins to appear in the market. For something that takes almost no time or effort to make, it tastes great.

This version makes a nice first course before a simple soup or stew supper. To make a meal of it on a hot day, try accompanying it with fresh bread or savory muffins, and plenty of iced mint tea.

The lemon-caper vinaigrette sauce is also lovely over rice and other steamed veggies. You can even make it ahead of time. Don't refrigerate it more than 24 hours, however. The garlic tends to get a bit strong, and the lemon juice loses its liveliness. Bring the sauce to room temperature before you use it.

Ingredients

1-½ pounds asparagus spears

¼ cup fresh lemon juice

1 tablespoon olive oil

3 tablespoons capers, drained (and chopped if large)

2 tablespoons finely chopped fresh parsley (or 2 teaspoons dried)

1 teaspoon minced garlic

Salt and freshly ground black pepper to taste

1. Boil water in your favorite steamer. Wash and trim the asparagus. If you want to be fancy, you can peel the stalks near the bottom. We don't usually bother, but if you don't like the fibrous outer coating getting stuck in your teeth, the extra work might be worth it to you. Put the asparagus in the steamer.

2. While you're waiting for the asparagus to get tender, vigorously whisk together the lemon juice and olive oil in a small bowl. Then whisk in the capers, parsley, garlic, and pepper.

3. When the asparagus is done to your liking, drain it well, then arrange on a plate and season to taste with salt and pepper. Drizzle the sauce over the asparagus and serve right away.

Ciambotta (Mixed Vegetable Stew)

Serves 4-6.

This grilled vegetable stew is a little more work than most of the recipes in this book because you grill the veggies first and then layer them into a casserole before you bake it. But if you can recruit a spouse or friend who likes to barbeque, they can help with the grilling part.

The finished product is definitely worth the small extra effort. It's an impressive dish to serve to company or to take to a pot luck. It's equally good piping hot, slightly warm, or at room temperature.

The broiling/grilling gives this stew a rich, slightly smoky flavor. So if you find yourself missing meat, just make this stew! If you can't get all the different colors of peppers, use two green and two red peppers. Just don't use all green peppers or the dish will taste different. Serve it with crusty bread and your best olive oil for dipping.

Ingredients

½ cup vegetable broth

1 tablespoon olive oil

1 medium eggplant, cut crosswise into ¼ inch slices

1-¼ pounds potatoes, cut into ¼ inch pieces

1 each - medium green, yellow, red, and orange bell peppers, seeded and cut crosswise into ¼ inch slices

1 medium zucchini, cut crosswise into ¼ inch slices

3 medium tomatoes, peeled, seeded and chopped

3 cloves garlic, chopped

¼ teaspoon salt

Freshly ground black pepper to taste

1. Spray a broiler rack or grill rack with nonstick cooking spray. Place it 5 inches from the heating element, and preheat the broiler or grill.

2. In a small bowl, whisk together the broth, oil, salt, and pepper.

3. With a pastry brush, lightly coat the eggplant, peppers, potatoes, and zucchini on both sides with the broth mixture.

4. Arrange the slices on the rack or grill. Broil or grill everything about 5 minutes, until tender and slightly charred.

5. Turn the vegetables over, and broil or grill 4 minutes more. Remove them to a plate.

6. Preheat the oven to 375 degrees.

7. Spray a 4 quart casserole with nonstick cooking spray.

8. Arrange the eggplant slices in the bottom of the casserole.

9. Sprinkle evenly with one-fourth of the tomatoes and garlic.

10. Add the potatoes, them top with another one-fourth of the tomatoes and garlic

11. Repeat with the peppers, and end with the zucchini, sprinkling each layer with another one-fourth of the tomatoes and garlic.

12. Bake, uncovered, 30-40 minutes, until bubbling. Serve hot, warm or at room temperature.

Italian Vegetable Stew with Cracked Wheat

2-3 generous servings.

This recipe is another one where you just cut up some vegetables, open some cans, and throw everything into a pot. The cracked wheat is an interesting and delicious addition. It adds a rich, almost meaty taste to the stew and thickens it nicely.

You can serve this stew over rice or with a crusty baguette to mop up the sauce.

Ingredients

2 tablespoons olive oil

½ cup chopped onion

3 garlic cloves, minced

1 medium zucchini, thinly sliced

4 ounces fresh mushrooms, sliced

½ teaspoon dried Italian Seasoning

¼ teaspoon crushed red pepper (more or less to taste)

1 14-½ ounce can diced tomatoes

1 8-ounce can tomato sauce

1 14-½-ounce can vegetable stock

¼ cup cracked wheat

½ of a 15-ounce can of kidney beans, drained and rinsed

⅛ cup fresh parsley

Shredded vegan mozzarella (optional)

1. Heat the oil in a large Dutch oven over medium-high heat.

2. Add the onion and garlic and sauté for 5 minutes.

3. Add the zucchini and mushrooms and cook for 5 another minutes.

4. Add the Italian Seasoning, crushed red pepper, tomatoes, tomato sauce, vegetable stock, and cracked wheat.

5. Bring to a boil, cover, reduce the heat, and simmer for about 30 minutes, until the cracked wheat is tender.

6. Stir in the kidney beans, green beans, and parsley. Simmer until heated through.

7. Serve hot, sprinkled with the shredded vegan cheese if desired.

Tomato, Bread, and Pasta Salad

Serves 4 –6.

This flavorful pasta salad includes dried bread cubes. It is a delicious way to use up leftover French or Ciabatta bread. You'll enjoy this dish on those hot summer days when you're really hungry from gardening, but don't want a hot meal.

This salad is best with fresh, vine-ripened tomatoes from your garden. If you're lucky enough to have access to a farmer's market, make this dish when good, juicy tomatoes are plentiful.

In the summer, we often cook up a bunch of pasta ahead of time and keep it refrigerated. If you do this and already have the pasta on hand, this salad takes almost no time to prepare.

Ingredients

3 cups of small dry pasta (such as shells or macaroni)

3 cups cut up tomato (about 1 ½ pounds)

⅓ cup olive oil

¼ cup chopped onion

1 clove garlic, minced

2 tablespoons chopped green olives

2 tablespoons balsamic vinegar

2 tablespoons chopped fresh basil, or 1 teaspoon dry

1 tablespoon chopped fresh parsley, or 1 teaspoon dry

¼ teaspoon freshly ground black pepper

½ teaspoon celery seed

½ teaspoon salt

About 1 cup cubed stale crusty bread, such as Ciabatta or French bread

1. Prepare the bread cubes by cutting up some leftover crusty bread. If it's gotten hard, that's okay. Let the bread dry out while you make everything else, or pop it into a toaster oven set at the lowest setting for a few minutes.

2. Mix everything except the pasta and bread in a big serving bowl and set it aside. You can do this step early in the day and put it in the refrigerator. Just make sure you stir it occasionally.

3. Cook the pasta according to package directions (or remove pre-cooked pasta from the refrigerator).

4. Rinse the pasta with cold water.

5. Add the pasta into the tomato mixture and toss until the pasta is coated with dressing.

6. Add the dried bread cubes, toss again, and eat.

Classic Glazed Carrots

Serves 4.

This simple dish emphasizes the sweetness of carrots. The secret is to cut the carrots into uniformly shaped pieces, so they cook as evenly as possible.

Cut the carrots into ¼-½ inch thick half rounds, depending on the width of the carrot. Make the pieces at the narrow end a little longer than the wider ones, so they don't overcook.

These carrots are perfect with Quick Vegan Stuffing (page 72) or Vegan Mashed Potatoes (page 53), and Real Gravy (page 12).

Ingredients

1-½ pounds carrots (preferably organic), peeled and chopped

2 tablespoons vegan margarine

1 tablespoon sugar

1-½ tablespoons flat leaf parsley, chopped

1 teaspoon chervil or chives, chopped

1. Cut the carrots in half lengthwise, then into half rounds. Place the carrots in a single layer in a large nonstick skillet. Add enough water to cover the carrots about halfway. Add the margarine and sugar, and bring to a boil over high heat.

2. Partially cover the skillet and reduce the heat to medium. Cook at a high simmer until the carrots are tender but not soft. Stir occasionally to coat the carrots with the cooking liquid.

3. Uncover and continue to cook until the liquid reduces to a thin syrup. Make sure you keep stirring, so nothing browns or burns. Toss the carrots with the parsley and herbs, and serve hot.

Sautéed Brussels Sprouts with Hazelnut Sauce

Serves 4.

This Brussels sprouts recipe is so tasty, some people may not even know they are eating brussels sprouts!

This sauce is too good not to use again and again. For example, you could substitute summer squash (cut in matchstick pieces) or French cut green beans for the Brussels sprouts. Make sure you adjust the cooking time accordingly, so you don't overcook the vegetables.

Ingredients

4 cups fresh Brussels sprouts

3 tablespoons vegan margarine

½ teaspoon salt

3 tablespoons red onion, chopped

1 cup vegetable stock (or a Morga cube dissolved in 1 cup boiling water)

1 teaspoon grated lemon zest

½ cup hazelnuts or filberts, toasted and chopped

1. Trim the Brussels sprouts and cut in half lengthwise. Then slice them into thin strips.

2. Heat the margarine in a non-stick skillet over medium heat. When melted, add the brussels sprouts, salt, and red onions. Cook until the sprout strips are just beginning to get tender (about 8 minutes).

3. Add the broth, and simmer for 7 minutes.

4. Stir in the lemon zest and hazelnuts. Serve immediately.

Brussels Sprouts with White Wine Sauce

Serves 2-4.

Even the most confirmed Brussels sprouts haters often will eat this dish because of the tasty sauce. For a special supper, serve these with Slow Roasted Tofu (page 170) and Quick Vegan Stuffing (page 72).

Ingredients

3 cups fresh Brussels sprouts

1 cup dry white wine

1 tablespoon vegan margarine

1 garlic clove, minced

1-½ teaspoons cornstarch

2 tablespoons cold water

½ teaspoon finely grated lemon peel

⅛ teaspoon white pepper

2 teaspoons fresh dill, minced

1. Trim the Brussels sprouts of excess stems and wilted outer leaves.

2. In a medium saucepan combine the brussels sprouts, white wine, margarine, and garlic. Bring to a boil. Reduce the heat and simmer for 7 to 10 minutes, or until the sprouts are nice and tender but not soft. Use a slotted spoon to remove the sprouts to a dish. Keep them warm.

3. Mix the cold water with the cornstarch, lemon peel, pepper, and dill.

4. Gradually add the lemon mixture to the hot wine in the saucepan. Cook and stir over medium heat until the mixture bubbles and thickens. Reduce the heat to a simmer, and stir for 2 minutes .

5. Pour the lemon sauce over the Brussels sprouts and serve.

Broccoli Tomato Salad

Serves 2-4.

This simple, elegant vegetable salad is good any time of the year. You could also use this salad as a sandwich filling for pitas or flour tortillas.

Ingredients

    5 cups broccoli florets

    1 pint cherry tomatoes, cut in half

    2 tablespoons chopped scallions (use only the white and tender green parts)

    ¼ cup vegan mayonnaise

    ¼ cup vegan sour cream

    1 tablespoon lemon juice

    1 teaspoon sugar

    ½ teaspoon sea salt

1. Steam the broccoli until it is tender yet still crisp, about 5-8 minutes. Drain it well, and put it into a large serving bowl to cool.

2. Meanwhile, whisk together the vegan mayonnaise, scallions, sour cream, lemon juice, sugar, and salt in a small bowl.

3. When the broccoli is cool, gently stir in the tomatoes and the scallion mixture.

4. Refrigerate for 1 hour and serve.

Sautéed Broccoli with Garlic and Lemon

Serves 2-4.

This nice, refreshing, low fat vegetable dish is for garlic lovers. Of course, you could reduce the amount of garlic, since six cloves is a lot! The idea is to have an intense garlic experience.

You could double the amount of wine, olive oil, margarine, and lemon juice, and serve this as a main dish with crusty French or Ciabatta bread, or with one of the rice pilafs in this book. This recipe would be equally good with green beans or sugar snap peas.

Ingredients

4 cups fresh broccoli florets

½ cup dry white wine

1 tablespoon extra virgin olive oil

1 teaspoon vegan margarine

6 garlic cloves, minced

¼ teaspoon salt

3 tablespoons fresh lemon juice

Freshly ground black pepper

1. Steam broccoli about 4 minutes, until barely tender.

2. In a large nonstick skillet, combine the broth, oil, and margarine over medium high heat.

3. Add the broccoli, garlic and salt. Cook, stirring frequently, about 8 minutes, until the broccoli is tender and some of the liquid has evaporated.

4. Transfer to a serving bowl, add the lemon juice, and mix. Serve warm or at room temperature.

Spicy White Bean Salad

Serves 4-6.

This recipe is a variation on the popular corn and black bean salad you often find on Mexican buffets. Substituting white beans makes this dish taste a bit richer and creamier, which makes it the perfect filling for warm soft flour tortillas. A little (or a lot) of vegan sour cream would be the perfect accompaniment. If you like hot peppers, you can add an additional jalapeno.

Ingredients

- 1 15-ounce can Great Northern beans, rinsed and drained
- 1 can crisp water-packed corn, rinsed and drained
- 1 medium red onion, diced
- 1 red bell pepper, seeded and diced
- 1 small fresh jalapeno pepper, seeded and sliced
- 1 clove garlic, minced fine
- 1 teaspoon sugar
- 2 tablespoons fresh lemon juice
- ½ teaspoon chili powder
- 2 tablespoons extra virgin olive oil
- 1 tablespoon white wine or rice wine vinegar
- ¼ teaspoon salt
- 2 tablespoons fresh cilantro, chopped

1. Combine all the ingredients in a large serving bowl and mix well.

2. Serve at room temperature as a side dish, or wrap in warm flour tortillas and eat as a snack, garnished with vegan sour cream.

Broccoli with Citrus Sauce

Serves 4.

If you'd like a delicious change from vegan hollandaise on your broccoli, try this unusual sauce. Citrus flavors compliment all green vegetables, so you could easily substitute green beans, sugar snap peas, or even steamed cabbage for the broccoli. This dish makes a nice light lunch in hot weather, with some good crusty French or Ciabatta bread to sop up the sauce. You could also serve this with a roasted potato dish, or alongside Quick Vegan Stuffing (page 72) topped with Real Gravy (page 12).

Ingredients

   1 pound broccoli florets

   1 tablespoon extra virgin olive oil

   2 tablespoons orange zest, grated

   1 tablespoon lemon zest, grated

   2 cloves garlic, minced

   ½ cup vegetable broth

   4 tablespoons vegan margarine

1. Steam the broccoli until it is crisp-tender, about 10 minutes. Drain it well and keep warm.

2. Meanwhile, heat the oil in a skillet over medium heat.

3. Add the orange zest, lemon zest, and garlic. Cook and stir 1 minute.

4. Add the broth and simmer 1 minute.

5. Add the margarine and cooked broccoli. Mix until the broccoli is hot and coated with the sauce, about 2 minutes.

6. Season with salt and freshly ground black pepper. Serve hot.

Garlicky Green Beans

Serves 4.

This unusual method of cooking the garlic in the green bean water gives you mellow, sweet garlic, without the fuss of roasting it. You could also make this with a pound of broccoli or cauliflower florets.

Serve this dish with one of the many roasted potato dishes in this book, with Tempeh Stroganoff (page 166), or with Vegan Mashed Potatoes (page 53) and Real Gravy (page 12).

Ingredients

1 pound fresh green beans, trimmed

2-3 whole garlic cloves, peeled

⅛ cup extra virgin olive oil

2-3 tablespoons balsamic vinegar

1 tablespoon white wine

½ teaspoon salt

¼ teaspoon freshly ground black pepper

1. Bring a big pot of salted water to a boil.

2. Add the beans and the whole garlic cloves. Boil for 5-7 minutes or until the beans are just barely tender. Drain the beans, and reserve the garlic cloves.

3. Place the beans in a serving bowl and keep them warm.

4. Whisk together the olive oil, balsamic vinegar, wine, salt, and freshly ground black pepper.

5. Mince the garlic cloves, then stir them into the mixture.

6. Drizzle the mixture over the beans, and toss. Serve hot or at room temperature.

Cupboard Three-Bean Salad

4 generous side dish servings.

This perennial favorite is easy to make from stuff you have on hand, and it's so much better than the store bought variety. Although the recipe might seem like it calls for lot of sugar, it's necessary to balance the vinegar and get that crisp sweet-sour taste. You can make this salad with fresh beans, instead of canned. Just trim about 2 cups each of green and yellow beans and steam them until they're slightly soft. (If the beans are too crisp, they won't absorb the marinade.)

Ingredients

1 15-ounce can yellow beans, drained and rinsed

1 15-ounce can green beans, drained and rinsed

1 15-ounce can red kidney beans, drained and rinsed

1 medium onion, diced

1 large green or red pepper, diced

¾ cup sugar

½ cup canola or mild olive oil

½ cup apple cider vinegar

1. Whisk the sugar, oil, and vinegar in a large non-reactive (glass or stainless steel) serving bowl.

2. Open the cans of beans, drain thoroughly, and add to the bowl. Toss until all the beans are coated with the dressing.

3. Store in the refrigerator for at least 4 hours. Take it out about 15 minutes before serving to give the oil a chance to loosen up. Stir well before serving.

Three-Bean Salad with Olives

Serves 6

This recipe is another "cupboard" salad. In other words, you can make it from things you already have in your refrigerator and pantry. If you do not have a red pepper handy, don't fret. This salad is excellent with just one green pepper. The pimentos in the olives add red pepper flavor. The dried oregano is essential however.

Ingredients

¼ cup olive oil

¼ cup white wine vinegar

1 tablespoon sugar

1-½ teaspoons dried oregano

1 teaspoon dried parsley

¼ teaspoon garlic powder

1 15-ounce can kidney beans, drained and rinsed

1 15-ounce can chickpeas, drained and rinsed

1 15-ounce can black-eyed peas, drained and rinsed

1 cup green bell pepper, chopped

1 cup red bell pepper, chopped

1 cup green olives stuffed with pimientos, sliced

½ cup red onion, chopped

Salt and freshly ground black pepper to taste

1. Whisk together the oil, vinegar, sugar, oregano, parsley, and garlic powder in a large serving bowl.

2. Add all the other ingredients except the salt and pepper. Mix well. Taste, then add salt and pepper as needed.

3. Cover and refrigerate 3 to 24 hours before serving.

Carrots Baked in Horseradish Cream

4 side-dish servings.

This tongue and soul-warming dish is the perfect easy recipe for winter weather. There's plenty of horseradish bite, which contrasts nicely with the sweetness of the carrots. It is outstanding as part of a holiday dinner.

If you want to save time peeling and cutting carrots, using a one-pound bag of pre-peeled baby organic snack carrots will work just fine. But with a little practice and a good vegetable peeler, you can prepare a pound of full-size carrots in a few minutes.

Organic carrots are easy to find, even in conventional grocery stores and we think they're worth the extra price. The flavor is far superior to the factory-farmed variety. If you don't believe us, taste a raw organic carrot alongside a non-organic one sometime, and you'll immediately see what we mean. Organic carrots are invariably much crisper and sweeter!

Ingredients

    1 pound small carrots, peeled and cut in half lengthwise

    ¼ cup vegan mayonnaise

    ¼ cup plain full fat soy milk (low fat will not give you a creamy sauce)

    ¼ cup freshly grated horseradish

    ¼ cup coarse fresh bread crumbs

    1 teaspoon melted vegan margarine

    Fresh parsley, chopped, for garnish (optional)

    Salt and freshly ground black pepper to taste

1. Preheat oven to 350 degrees.

2. Place the carrots in a saucepan with just enough water to cover them. Bring to a boil, then cook until they are tender when pierced with a fork (around 10 minutes).

3. Reserve ¼ cup of the carrot cooking water, and drain the rest. Set the carrots aside.

4. In a mixing bowl, whisk the reserved water, mayonnaise, milk and horseradish together until smooth. Add the salt and freshly ground pepper to taste.

5. Spread the carrots out in a 9 by 13 inch baking dish. Pour the sauce over them.

6. Moisten the bread crumbs with the melted butter, then sprinkle them over the carrot mixture.

7. Place the pan on the center oven rack, and bake until the bread crumbs are toasted, about 7-10 minutes.

8. Garnish the dish with fresh chopped parsley. Serve immediately, straight out of the oven.

Summer Squash Baked with Cherry Tomatoes, Olives and Fresh Thyme

Serves 2.

For this dish, you just throw everything into a pan. Then you can go relax and sip a nice glass of wine while it bakes. Good crusty bread would not be amiss here, and if you'd like to do an all-oven meal, you could start Mustard Roasted Potatoes with Herbs (page 44) about 15 minutes before you put this dish into the oven.

This dish is easily doubled or tripled for company and is a nice way to turn the inevitable surplus of squash from your garden into a Mediterranean treat. You may use Kalamata olives instead of mild black ones, but make sure you pit and rinse them before adding them. If you don't, their brininess will permeate the dish.

You may also add a generous ¼ cup of chopped fresh herbs instead of the thyme. Basil or marjoram would work well. For an exotic twist try two tablespoons of chopped fresh pineapple sage or a tablespoon of mint.

Ingredients

1-½ pounds any type of summer squash, or a mixture (such as zucchini or crookneck), cut into ½ inch thick slices

2 cups halved or quartered cherry tomatoes

15 black olives, halved

¼ cup olive oil

¼ pound shredded or finely chopped vegan mozzarella

3 tablespoons minced garlic

2 teaspoons finely chopped fresh thyme leaves (or 2 tablespoons chopped fresh parsley and ¼ teaspoon dried thyme)

1. Preheat oven to 425 degrees.

2. Combine the olive oil, minced garlic, and thyme leaves in an 9 x 13 inch baking dish.

3. Add the halved cherry tomatoes, black olives, and summer squash cut into ½-inch thick slices. Stir so everything is coated and mixed.

4. Sprinkle with the vegan cheese, place in the oven on the center rack and bake for 20 to 25 minutes.

Baked Eggplant

Serves 4.

When properly prepared and cooked, eggplant is one of the most luscious vegetables around. The secret to making delicious eggplant is to salt the slices and let them stand for about 30 minutes before cooking. Wipe off the salt then sauté, grill, broil, or bake.

People used to perform the eggplant salting ritual to remove the bitterness from the eggplant, but contemporary varieties rarely taste bitter. The real reason to salt the eggplant is to extract some of the liquid, which makes the eggplant firmer, so it absorbs far less oil during cooking.

We love breaded eggplant, but this version is much easier, just as tasty, and lower in fat. For a complete meal, you could serve these slices alongside Middle Eastern Rice Pilaf (page 68) and a spinach salad dressed with a little good olive oil, some salt and pepper, and some slivered almonds or pine nuts.

See the Vegan Sandwiches chapter for some other ways to use these baked eggplant slices.

Ingredients

    1 large eggplant (about 1 pound), or 2 or 3 smaller eggplants

    Sea salt

    6 tablespoons fruity olive oil

    2 tablespoons tamari

    1 tablespoon poultry seasoning (or 1-½ teaspoons sage, ½ teaspoon thyme, ½ teaspoon marjoram, and ½ teaspoon black pepper)

    1 teaspoon sugar

1. If the eggplant has been waxed, peel it. If not, wash it well and dry it completely. Slice the eggplant into rounds that are about ¼ inch thick.

2. Lay the eggplant slices in a single layer on some plates. Sprinkle liberally with sea salt.

3. Let the slices sit for about 30-60 minutes. Wipe off the salt with a moist paper towel.

4. Preheat the oven to 400 degrees. Spray a cookie sheet with nonstick canola oil spray.

5. Whisk the olive oil, tamari, poultry seasoning, and sugar in a small bowl until completely blended.

6. Arrange the eggplant slices in a single layer on the cookie sheet. Brush them lightly with the oil mixture, and put the eggplant into the hot oven.

7. Bake about 15-20 minutes or until the eggplant is nice and tender. Baste the slices every few minutes with the oil mixture.

8. Serve right away. To save it for later sandwiches, cool the slices, wrap them tightly in plastic wrap or foil and store in the refrigerator.

Baba Eggplant

Serves 4.

This recipe is best made on a grill whether a miniature stovetop indoor grill or an outdoor charcoal or gas grill.

Although it's just as easy to make, Baba Eggplant is much spicier than the basic Baked Eggplant (page 98) because it adds garlic, herbs, and allspice.

For an extra special presentation, top each slice with a creamy dressing. Just mix a small container of plain soy yogurt with a teaspoon of dried mint, a teaspoon of honey, and a teaspoon of dried thyme. Put a tiny dollop of dressing on each eggplant slice and serve it with Middle Eastern Pilaf (page 68) and some steamed spinach.

Ingredients

1 large eggplant (about 1 pound) or 2 - 3 smaller eggplants

Sea salt

6 tablespoons fruity olive oil

4 cloves garlic, minced

1 teaspoon dried oregano

1 teaspoon ground cumin

½ teaspoon dried mint, crumbled into a powder

½ teaspoon ground allspice

1 teaspoon sugar

1. Preheat an indoor grill or prepare an outdoor grill.

2. If the eggplant has been waxed, peel it. If not, wash it well and dry it completely. Slice the eggplant into rounds that are about ¼ inch thick.

3. Lay the eggplant slices in a single layer on some plates. Sprinkle liberally with sea salt.

4. Let the slices sit for about 30-60 minutes. Wipe off the salt with a moist paper towel.

5. Preheat the oven to 400 degrees. Spray a cookie sheet with nonstick canola oil spray.

6. Whisk the olive oil, garlic, herbs and spices, and sugar in a small bowl until it is completely blended.

7. Oil the grill rack. Arrange the eggplant slices on the rack, brush with the oil mixture, and put over the heat.

8. Grill about 15 minutes or until the eggplant is nice and tender, basting every few minutes with the oil mixture.

9. When done, serve right away. To store, cool the slices and wrap them tightly in plastic wrap or foil. Store them in the refrigerator for wraps and pita sandwiches.

Sweet Potato Chili Stew

Serves 4 as a side dish.

This stew is extremely easy. You just cut things up and nuke them in the microwave. The flavor is terrific, with chili powder and earthy black beans balancing the sweetness of the yams, honey, and juice.

This dish is also extremely low in fat, high in fiber and protein, and full of beta-carotene. (It's nice when something so healthy is also yummy!) Sweet potatoes team up nicely with all sort of chili flavors, so experiment with different types of chili powders.

You can even try substituting garam masala for the chili powder, to create an East Indian version of the dish. In that case, add a little chopped fresh cilantro at the end for an unusual and delicious combination.

You can serve this recipe as a main dish by piling it into soft flour tortillas and adding a dollop of vegan sour cream, some shredded spinach leaves, and a sprinkle of Tabasco.

Ingredients

- 1 cup chopped yellow onion
- 1 tablespoon chili powder
- 1 cup orange juice
- 1 cup water
- 1 tablespoon honey
- Salt to taste
- 2 pounds sweet potatoes, peeled and cut into 1 inch chunks
- 2 teaspoons soft vegan margarine
- 2 teaspoons flour
- 1 15-ounce can black beans, drained and rinsed
- Optional - ¼ cup toasted almond slivers

1. Put the onions, chili powder, orange juice, water, honey, salt and sweet potatoes in a large, microwave-safe bowl. Cover and microwave on high power, about 20 minutes, stirring once or until the potatoes are done but still hold their shape.

2. Stir in the beans. Blend the butter and flour and add to mixture.

3. Cover, microwave on high power for 5 minutes more, or until the beans are heated through and the stew has thickened slightly.

4. Sprinkle with almonds, if desired.

Acorn Squash with Mushrooms and Onions

Serves 6.

This comforting, satisfying cold weather dish looks impressive on a holiday table and gets rave reviews. The homey taste of onions and mushrooms works beautifully with the slightly sweet, earthy squash.

You can adjust the amounts in this recipe up or down. Because it's flexible, you can easily serve two people by baking just one squash and using a small onion and a handful of mushrooms.

For an easy party dish, partially bake the squash, stuff them, and refrigerate them overnight. They can even go straight from the fridge to a baking pan or cookie sheet. Just increase the second baking time for 5-10 minutes.

When baking any kind of winter squash, line the pan with foil first. Most winter squash have a high sugar content. If they ooze some liquid, you could end up with a tough clean up job.

Ingredients

3 acorn squash

2 cups onions, chopped

1 6-ounce can of mushrooms or 8 ounces of chopped fresh mushrooms

Vegan margarine

Salt to taste

Freshly ground black pepper to taste

1. Cut the squash in half and remove the seeds. Put several generous dabs of vegan margarine in each half. Place the squash on a cookie sheet lined with foil, and bake at 350 degrees for 30-35 minutes.

2. Meanwhile, sauté the onions and mushrooms in a little vegan margarine until they are slightly softened and the mushrooms are no longer giving off moisture.

3. Remove the squash from the oven, allow to cool for about 10 minutes, and dab in more margarine. Sprinkle with salt and pepper. Then stuff each half with the onion and mushroom mixture. At this point, you can let the squash cool completely, wrap them tightly, and refrigerate.

4. To finish the dish, bake the squash in a 350 degree oven for 20-30 minutes until the squash are tender when pierced with a fork.

Spinach Seasoned with Soy, Sesame and Garlic

2 servings as a main dish salad with rice or soba noodles.

This recipe is simple, but good. Spinach marries well with Far Eastern flavors like sesame and soy. Warm or cold, it's the perfect make-ahead accompaniment for an Asian-influenced stew or curry.

Although it may seem like a lot of spinach, it shrinks! You can easily halve this recipe to serve one person (or two as a side dish).

This recipe is delicious with plain jasmine rice, and hot green or genmai cha (roasted brown rice tea).

Ingredients

2 10 ounce packages fresh spinach

¼ cup scallions, finely chopped

1 teaspoon sesame seeds

2 teaspoons low sodium soy sauce or tamari

½ teaspoon dark sesame oil

¼ teaspoon kosher salt

2 cloves garlic, minced

1. In a small bowl, whisk together all the ingredients except the spinach.

2. Steam the spinach until it wilts, about 5 minutes. (Steam it in batches if necessary.)

3. Let the spinach cool slightly, then squeeze it dry.

4. Combine the spinach and the dressing, tossing it thoroughly to combine.

5. Serve chilled or at room temperature.

Squash and Green Bean Medley

Serves 2.

This simple recipe is great if you have a garden. Every gardener knows that green beans and summer squash are easy to grow. That means sometime in the summer, you'll have an overabundance of them because generally when they're ready, they're ready in *volume*. (With this recipe, you can use up some of them anyway.)

Ingredients

1 pound green beans, chopped

2 large yellow squash (golden bar or crookneck), cut lengthwise into quarters and then into ½-inch slices

2 tablespoons vegan margarine

1 teaspoon olive oil

1 teaspoon Italian seasoning

1 teaspoon garlic salt

½ teaspoon black pepper

⅓ cup water

1 tomato, chopped

1. Place the water and the green beans in a skillet and cook over medium heat until the beans are slightly tender, about 8 minutes.

2. Add the margarine and oil to the pan.

3. After the margarine melts, add squash, Italian seasoning, garlic salt, and pepper. Cook over medium heat until some of the squash becomes slightly translucent.

4. Add chopped tomato to mixture, stir, and serve as a side dish or over rice or couscous.

Skillet Carrot and Turnip Stew

Serves 4.

Turnips are delicious; they are somewhat like a potato with a touch of earthy sweetness. This recipe takes advantage of turnips' natural affinity for other root vegetables, such as carrots and onions. Although the stew is a great side dish, you also could split it with a friend, and adding a salad of mixed greens to round out the meal.

Ingredients

 1-½ tablespoons extra virgin olive oil

 1-½ tablespoons vegan margarine

 1 medium onion, sliced in rings

 1 pound turnips, peeled and cut into ½ inch chunks

 ¾ pound carrots, peeled and sliced into ½ inch rounds

 Salt and freshly ground pepper to taste

 1 tablespoon coarsely chopped fresh tarragon or basil (or 1 teaspoon dried)

 1 14-ounce can diced tomatoes, preferably organic, drained

 2 tablespoons chopped fresh flat leaf parsley

1. Heat the margarine and olive oil in a large nonstick skillet over medium high heat.

2. Add the onions, turnips, and carrots. Saute for 2 minutes, then add salt to taste and cover. Reduce the heat to medium low and cook for 5 minutes.

3. Uncover and cook over medium-low heat, stirring occasionally, until the carrots and turnips are almost tender and are just beginning to brown, about 15-20 minutes.

4. Reduce the heat to low, add the tarragon or basil, stir in the drained diced tomatoes and simmer another 5-10 minutes.

5. Top with fresh chopped parsley before serving.

Veggie Faux-Hamburger Bake

Serves 4.

This recipe is the ultimate in winter comfort food. It's reminiscent of one of those Hamburger Helper casseroles Mom used to make back in the 60s, before we all realized what is actually *in* those boxes of prefab food. This dish has all the taste without the creepy chemicals or cholesterol.

Ingredients

   1 15-ounce can chopped tomatoes

   1 head of cauliflower or broccoli

   ½ cup bulgur wheat

   ¼ cup water

   ¼ cup wine

   pepper and salt to taste

   5 slices bread, toasted

   2-3 tablespoon vegan "cheese"

   ¼ cup nutritional yeast

   1 package vegan "ground round"

   1 tablespoon olive oil

1. Preheat oven to 350 degrees. Mix tomatoes, cauliflower or broccoli, bulgur, water, wine, salt, and pepper in a 9 x 13 pan. Place in preheated oven and bake for 35 minutes.

2. While the mixture bakes, make breadcrumbs. First toast the bread slices. Then cut into cubes and put into a blender or food processor. Pulse to create crumbs.

3. Place the bread crumbs in a bowl and mix with the cheese and nutritional yeast.

4. Remove the pan from the oven and increase the temperature to 400 degrees. Mix in the ground round and sprinkle the bread crumb mixture on top. Drizzle olive oil on the crumbs.

5. Return the pan to the oven and bake another 20 minutes until the topping is golden brown. Serve immediately.

Easy Broccoli Casserole

Serves 4.

We often like to make food you can sort of forget about while you do other things. Although this casserole takes a while because it bakes, you don't have to pay attention to it. First make the rice and forget about that for 20 minutes or so. Then chop and cook the broccoli and onion, blend the sauce, and finally dump everything into the oven.

Ingredients

  1 box long grain and wild rice

  1 onion

  1 tablespoon oil

  2 bunches of broccoli, chopped

  2 tablespoons water

  1 silken tofu

  ½ cup nutritional yeast

  1 tablespoon lemon juice

  ¾ cup water

  1 teaspoon garlic granules

  1 teaspoon garlic salt

1. Prepare rice according to package directions.

2. Preheat the oven to 350 degrees. Put oil in pan, heat over medium heat, and add onion. Cook the onion until it is translucent.

3. Add the broccoli and 2 tablespoons water to the pan, and turn down the heat to medium-low. Cover and steam for about five minutes until the broccoli is bright green.

4. In a blender or food processor, blend the tofu, nutritional yeast, lemon juice, water, garlic granules, and garlic salt.

5. In a big bowl, stir the onion/broccoli mixture together with the rice and the tofu sauce. Put the mixture in a 9 x 13 pan and bake for 30 minutes.

Curried Potatoes and Cauliflower with Cream Cheese

Serves 4.

If you like creamy potatoes, you'll like this recipe. It is somewhat reminiscent of scalloped potatoes, but without the high fat content. The cauliflower adds some extra flavor too. Even people who don't like that particular cruciferous vegetable probably won't object to it in this dish because it blends in so nicely with the other creamy flavors and spices.

Ingredients

1 pound cauliflower, chopped (1 head)

1 pound potatoes (about 4 medium)

3 tablespoons margarine

2 teaspoons curry powder

1 teaspoon sage

½ teaspoon paprika

¼ teaspoon garlic powder (or asafetida)

1 teaspoon salt

¼ teaspoon black pepper

3-4 tablespoon vegan cream cheese

2 tablespoons salsa

½ cup soymilk

½ cup water

2 teaspoons flour

1. Wash and cut potatoes and cauliflower. Place in steamer with 2 cups of water and steam for 20-25 minutes until the potatoes are tender. Drain and set aside.

2. Combine the margarine, curry powder, sage, paprika, and garlic powder (or asafetida) in pan on medium heat to toast the spices.

3. Add the salt, black pepper, cream cheese, salsa, milk, and water to the pan and mix with toasted spices. Add flour and stir to thicken.

4. Place sauce and vegetables in a big bowl and stir to mix. Serve immediately.

Vegan Sandwiches

You might wonder how it's possible to make a decent sandwich without meat or cheese. But here are a bunch of 100% vegan sandwiches to satisfy even the most confirmed meat lover. Some of the sandwiches are high in protein, and others are lighter and feature vegetables. We've also included a few tortilla-based goodies and a couple of unusual combinations that can become addictive.

Of course, nothing is easier than throwing together a sandwich. All you need is decent bread, a few goodies to stick inside of it, and your two hands to eat it. Nearly all of these sandwiches make good brown bag lunches and can be eaten on the run.

If you've been trying to find vegan sandwiches that kids will enjoy, a number of these taste familiar and homey. There are even some vegan versions of classic favorites, like the club sandwich and PB and J.

We have also included a few recipes for bread spreads, including a couple of homemade vegan mayonnaise recipes. If you can find it, Vegenaise is an excellent mayonnaise that has a long shelf life, contains no eggs or trans fats, and tastes familiar, like a good quality commercial mayonnaise. If it's not available in your area, you can easily make an excellent mayo substitute yourself (see page 135 or 136).

Vegan Nut Butter and Fruit Spread Sandwiches

Makes 1 sandwich.

Here are four delicious variations on the timeless peanut butter and jelly theme. Kids of all ages like these sandwiches. Note the all-important method of putting the sandwich together. Of course, you could do it the conventional way, spreading the jam on top of the nut butter. But it's not the same as glomming two thickly spread hunks of bread together, is it?

Linzer Sandwich

   2 slices whole grain or sprouted grain bread

   1-2 tablespoons roasted almond butter

   2 tablespoons seedless raspberry jam or fruit spread

1. Spread one slice of bread with almond butter and one slice with raspberry jam.

2. Press the two slices together. Enjoy!

Banana Soy Nut Sandwich

   2 slices whole grain or sprouted grain bread

   1-2 tablespoons crunchy soy butter

   1 banana (ripe or not, both kinds work)

   2 teaspoons honey

1. Spread one slice of bread with the soy butter the other with the honey.

2. Slice the banana into thick slices, and arrange on top of the soy butter. Lay the slice with honey on top of the slice with the banana.

Taffy Apple Sandwich

    2 slices whole grain or sprouted grain bread

    1-2 tablespoons crunchy all natural peanut butter

    1 tablespoon honey roasted peanuts, crushed

    1-2 tablespoons apple butter

1. Spread one slice of bread with the peanut butter. Sprinkle the nuts on it.

2. Spread the other slice with a thick layer of apple butter. Press the slices together.

This sandwich is great accompanied with hot apple cider that you stir with a cinnamon stick.

Coffee Cake Sandwich

    2 slices whole grain or sprouted grain bread

    1-2 tablespoons cashew butter

    1 tablespoon chopped pecans

    2 tablespoons apricot, strawberry, or peach preserves

1. Spread one slice of bread with the cashew butter, and top with pecans.

2. Spread the other slice with your choice of preserves, and press the two slices together.

This sandwich makes a lovely breakfast with café au lait.

Vegan Club Sandwich

Serves 1.

When you have leftover tofu, a sandwich just doesn't get any easier than this one. The success of this sandwich is in the ingredients: the better the bread, the riper the tomato, the crisper the lettuce, the better the sandwich. If you don't have leftover tofu, you also could use one of the many packaged pre-baked tofu slices that are available.

If you want to boost the protein content, you also could bake or fry a vegan bacon substitute. (These are often available in the refrigerated or frozen section of natural food stores.) But adding the vegan bacon bits works well too, and imparts a nice crunch to this sandwich, which is satisfying.

For a hearty cold or wet weather meal, you could pair this sandwich with California Carrot Soup page 142).

Ingredients

2 Chicken Fried Tofu Cutlets (page 158) or 2 slices Slow Roasted Tofu (page 170)

3 slices fresh bread of your choice (or 1 small baguette, split)

2 tablespoons vegan mayonnaise

1 tablespoon vegan bacon bits

2-3 thick slices ripe tomato

A leaf or two of romaine lettuce

1. Warm the tofu cutlets in the microwave on medium for about 20 seconds.

2. Lightly toast the bread slices, or warm the baguette for about 1 minute in a toaster oven.

3. Mix the vegan mayonnaise and the fake bacon bits together in a small bowl. Spread a little on each slice of toast, or on each cut side of the baguette.

4. Place the tofu slices on one slice of bread. Cover with the second slice.

5. Arrange the tomatoes and lettuce on top. Cover with the last slice, spread side down of course.

6. Slice in halves or quarters, and enjoy.

Cold Eggplant Sandwich

1 sandwich.

This sandwich is extremely easy if you've already made extra Baked Eggplant (page 100). Eggplant is delicious cold, so a sandwich is a great way to use leftover eggplant slices.

This sandwich is good with beer, wine, or iced coffee with some cinnamon or nutmeg added.

Ingredients

  1 individual baguette, or an 8-inch section of a large baguette, split

  2-3 slices of cold Baked Eggplant (page 98)

  2 tablespoons vegan mayonnaise

  1 tablespoon chopped fresh cilantro

  ¼ teaspoon sea salt

  1 teaspoon hot garlic-chili paste

  2-3 slices fresh tomato

  1 very thin slice of raw red onion

1. Split the bread lengthwise. Mix the vegan mayonnaise, cilantro, salt, and chili paste with a fork until well blended.

2. Spread both sides of the bread with the spicy mayonnaise.

3. Lay the eggplant slices on one cut side of the bread, top with the tomatoes and onions. Cover with the other slice of bread.

4. Cut in half and eat.

Hot Eggplant Sandwich

1 sandwich.

This recipe is a decadent vegan version of the classic Italian breaded eggplant sandwich with cheese and tomato sauce. This sandwich is just as rich and satisfying as the original without the dairy products.

Ingredients

1 individual baguette, or an 8-inch section of a large baguette, split

2-3 slices of cold Baked Eggplant (page 98) or Baba Eggplant (page 100)

1 clove garlic, minced

½ teaspoon dried oregano

2 tablespoons vegan cream cheese

4 tablespoons prepared tomato sauce, such as Hearty Vegan Tomato Sauce (page 14)

1 very thin slice raw red onion

1. Preheat the oven to 375 degrees.

2. Split the bread lengthwise. In a small bowl, mix the garlic, oregano, and vegan cream cheese with a fork until well blended.

3. Spread both sides of the bread with the cream cheese mixture.

4. Lay the eggplant slices on one cut side of the bread, and spread the tomato sauce on the slices. Add the onion slice and cover with the other slice of bread.

5. Wrap the sandwich very tightly in aluminum foil, and place in the hot oven. Bake for about 5-10 minutes, until the sandwich is very hot and oozing with sauce.

Reubenesque Vegan Sandwich

1 sandwich.

Although this sandwich isn't quite like a real Rueben Sandwich, it's awfully good. Virtually all artisan rye and pumpernickel breads are vegan. A real European baker would never dream of putting stuff like whey or dry milk into a rye bread (but read the labels to be sure).

This sandwich is not exactly low fat. But it still has a lot less fat than the original, which is filled with meat and dairy.

The small amount of raw cashew butter adds a subtle flavor that may remind you of Swiss cheese. That along with the Thousand Island Dressing (page 22), makes this sandwich something special. Of course, you'd never find raw onion in a traditional Reuben, but it's still really delicious.

Ingredients

2 slices rye or pumpernickel bread (seeded or not)

2 teaspoons (or less) raw cashew butter

2 tablespoons vegan cream cheese

1 tablespoon vegan bacon bits

2 tablespoon drained sauerkraut

2 tablespoons Thousand Island Dressing (page 22)

1 thin slice raw red onion, divided into rings

1 tablespoon vegan margarine

1. Take the bread slices and lay them out flat. Spread a small amount of cashew butter on each slice.

2. Mix the vegan cream cheese and bacon bits in a small bowl, then spread on one slice of bread.

3. Spread Thousand Island Dressing over the cream cheese and bacon bits. Lay the drained sauerkraut on top and top with red onion rings and the second slice of bread.

4. Heat half the vegan margarine in a nonstick skillet over medium high heat until it bubbles. Lay the sandwich in the pan, reduce the heat, and cook about 3 minutes (watch carefully, so it doesn't burn). Add the rest of the vegan margarine, flip the sandwich, and cook until it's nice and crisp, another few minutes. Serve immediately.

Vegan Cream Cheese Sandwiches

1 sandwich.

There are two vegan substitutes that you simply cannot make successfully at home without going to enormous trouble: cheese and ice cream. So for this sandwich, and its variations, you'll need to lay your hands on some good vegan cream cheese.

Make these sandwiches on a hot day or for a special "high tea" treat. The sandwiches also go very nicely with soup.

Ingredients

2 thin slices whole grain pumpernickel or sourdough bread

½ cup vegan cream cheese

Coarsely ground sea salt and freshly ground pepper

1 teaspoon fresh thyme leaves

8 thin slices cucumber

1 thin slice red onion

2 tablespoons grated carrot

2 tablespoons clover sprouts

1. If you want to get fancy, trim the crusts from the bread. (We don't.)

2. Spread each slice with the cream cheese, and sprinkle with salt, pepper, and the thyme leaves.

3. Lay the cucumber on top of one slice of bread, followed by the onion, carrot, and sprouts. Cover with the other slice of bread.

Variations

Cream Cheese and Tomato: Substitute 4 fat slices of juicy beefsteak tomato for the cucumber, and 2 tablespoons chopped fresh basil for the thyme. Keep the onion, but omit the carrots and sprouts.

Cream Cheese and Radish: Substitute 2 thinly sliced radishes sprinkled with a little white wine vinegar for the cucumber. Keep the onion and sprouts, but omit the carrots.

Cream Cheese, Bacon, and Roasted Red Pepper: Mix the cream cheese with 2 tablespoons vegan bacon bits. Instead of cucumber, substitute some roasted red peppers from a jar (well-drained). Basil or thyme are both good additions as is a little chopped fresh tarragon. You also can omit the carrot and other veggies if you wish.

Vegan BLT

1 sandwich.

Unlike a real bacon, lettuce and tomato (BLT) sandwich, this vegan version doesn't include all the fatty nitrate-laden stuff. But you will be surprised at how well this sandwich can satisfy your craving for one of the all-time great culinary inventions: the BLT. Plus this BLT is a whole lot easier and less messy, since there's no frying bacon!

If you can't find vegan bacon, dulse makes a good alternative. Just lightly sauté it in a pan, so it gets a little crunchy. If you've never heard of it, dulse is dried seaweed that comes in sheets. Although it doesn't really taste like bacon per se, it gives the sandwich a remarkably bacon-y quality. Plus, dulse is loaded with B vitamins, so unlike bacon, it's actually *good* for you.

Ingredients

2 thick slices whole grain bread

1-2 tablespoons vegan mayonnaise (we like Vegenaise, or see the recipes later in this section)

2 slices juicy, ripe tomato

2 tablespoons vegan bacon bits, 2 slices sautéed vegan bacon strips, or dulse.

1 slice crisp romaine lettuce

1. Lightly toast the bread and spread both slices with the mayonnaise.

2. Arrange the tomatoes on top, sprinkle with bacon bits (or lay the bacon or dulse strips on top).

3. Top with lettuce and the other slice of bread, and enjoy.

English Style Mushroom Sandwich

1 sandwich.

Pubs in England often serve a version of this sandwich. Although it seems deceptively simple, try this sandwich with a cold beer or a glass of crisp white wine, and you'll be hooked. Vegan Worcester sauce adds some zip to this delicious sandwich.

Ingredients

    4 ounces thinly sliced white mushrooms

    1 teaspoon Worcester sauce (or more to taste)

    1 teaspoon drived chives, or 1 tablespoon fresh minced chives

    2 tablespoons vegan margarine, divided

    2 slices white, wheat or potato bread (fairly soft bread is best)

1. Heat 1 tablespoon margarine in a nonstick skillet over medium heat until melted.

2. Add the mushrooms and dried chives (if using), and sauté very gently, stirring a few times, until the mushrooms start to release some liquid (about 3-4 minutes). Stir in the Worcester Sauce. Set aside and keep warm.

3. Add the other tablespoon of margarine to the pan over medium high heat. Add the bread slices and cook until they are nice and brown on one side.

4. Place one slice of bread, uncooked side up, on a plate. Pile on the mushroom mixture. Top with the second slice of bread, cooked side up, and serve immediately.

Vegan Quesadillas

Makes 2.

Even though good vegan cheeses exist, they generally don't make good quesadillas because vegan cheeses don't really melt well.

The answer? Vegan cream cheese!

Just spread a thin layer of vegan cream cheese on your tortillas, add all your other goodies, and enjoy yourself! Serve these tasty treats with iced tea spiked with a little lime, a good cold beer, or margaritas.

Ingredients

4 flour or corn tortillas, your choice

½ cup vegan cream cheese

1 can fat free refried beans, preferably organic

½ cup canned corn, drained well

½ cup chopped onion

½ cup fresh spinach, chopped

1 fresh jalapeno pepper, seeded and chopped

½ cup of your favorite salsa

1 teaspoon ground cumin

1 teaspoon chili powder

Olive oil for frying

1. Heat a little olive oil in a non-stick skillet over medium heat.

2. Use two tortillas per person. Spread one with ½ of the vegan cream cheese. Pile on the corn, onion, spinach, jalapeno, and salsa. Spread the other tortilla with some of the refried beans, and sandwich them together.

3. Carefully place the quesadilla in the pan of oil, and fry gently on medium heat, about 4 minutes per side, until crisp. If you are using corn tortillas, flipping the quesadilla will be tricky because the edges tend to curl up. If that's the case, use two spatulas, and do the best you can!

Potato Wraps

10 sandwiches.

To make this unusual, satisfying wrap sandwich, you'll need to make Blender Hummus (page 134). Store bought hummus would also work, but the homemade variety is especially good in this wrap. Read the labels of taco seasoning carefully. Some contain all kinds of weird stuff, including MSG.

Ingredients

8 medium russet potatoes, peeled and shredded

2 teaspoons extra virgin olive oil

10 organic flour tortillas

2 cups Blender Hummus (page 134)

2 tablespoons taco seasoning

1 large Haas avocado, peeled, pitted, and diced

2 cups red onion, chopped

2 cups shredded lettuce

1. Heat the olive oil over medium heat in a large nonstick skillet, and spread the shredded potatoes evenly in the pan. Turn the heat up to medium high, and cook for about 3-4 minutes, until the potatoes start to brown. Turn them over, and cook another 3 minutes or so, until tender.

2. Warm the tortillas (you can wrap them in foil and pop them in the toaster oven for a few minutes). Spread each tortilla with some hummus. Sprinkle with taco seasoning, add some potatoes, then a little avocado, onion, and lettuce.

3. Roll tortillas up tightly. Serve right away, or store in the refrigerator wrapped in plastic wrap. Bring to room temperature before serving.

Curried Eggless Egg Salad Sandwiches

Enough filling for about 6 sandwiches.

This savory, addictive, high protein sandwich filling is perfect for lunchboxes. You can use it to fill pitas, flour tortillas, split sprouted grain buns, or even mound some on Vegan Biscuit halves (page 26) to make hor d'oeuvres.

Vary the amount of raw vegetables to suit your taste. We like a lot of veggies, but if you want a more traditional consistency, cut back on the veggies by about half.

Ingredients

12-ounces extra firm tofu, drained and mashed

½ cup vegan mayonnaise

¼ cup pickle relish, drained

½ medium sweet onion, minced or 1 teaspoon onion powder

2 stalks celery, chopped fine

2 carrots, chopped very fine or shredded

½ medium green or red pepper, seeded and chopped very fine

1 tablespoon yellow curry powder

½ teaspoon garlic powder

1 teaspoon sea salt

½ teaspoon sweet paprika

Pinch cayenne pepper

12 slices bread, your choice (our favorite is sourdough)

Put everything except the bread in a big bowl, mix thoroughly, and refrigerate about an hour before filling sandwiches.

Blender Hummus

Scant 2 cups of filling.

The secret to this hummus is to simmer the canned chickpeas for about 15 minutes before blending them. Otherwise your hummus will be somewhat dry and grainy. It will still be good, but it won't have a nice soft consistency.

Ingredients

1 15-ounce can chickpeas, with liquid

2 cloves garlic, pressed

2 tablespoons tamari

Juice of 1 lemon

½ cup tahini (sesame paste)

2 tablespoons chopped cilantro

Extra virgin olive oil (optional)

1. Put the chickpeas and their liquid in a small saucepan. If necessary, add enough water to cover the chickpeas. Heat until boiling, then reduce heat to a high simmer and cook for 10-15 minutes. Drain and cool the chickpeas.

2. Put the cooled chickpeas, garlic, tamari, lemon juice, tahini, and cilantro into a blender or food processor. Process until smooth, scraping down the sides of bowl. If you wish, add a tablespoon or so of extra virgin olive oil if the hummus is too thick.

3. Store in the refrigerator for up to a week (though it probably won't last that long).

Vegan Mayonnaise

About 1-½ cups.

Although this vegan version of mayonnaise doesn't have the long shelf life of commercial mayonnaise, its flavor is fresh and lively. Don't just use this mayo for sandwiches. Thinned with a little soy milk and olive oil, it makes an excellent light sauce for steamed or grilled vegetables, especially if you add some chopped fresh herbs.

Ingredients

- ½ cup plain full fat soy milk
- 1-½ teaspoons sea salt
- ½ teaspoon onion powder
- ¼ teaspoon garlic powder
- 1 tablespoon Dijon mustard
- ½ - 1 teaspoon sugar
- 1 tablespoon white wine or apple cider vinegar
- 1 cup safflower, sunflower, or canola oil

1. Measure all of the ingredients except the oil into blender, food processor with steel blade, or a Kitchen Aid mixer with a whip attachment.
2. Blend on medium speed and slowly add the oil drop by drop.
3. Once the mixture starts to thicken, you can add the oil a little faster, in a trickle.
4. Keep mixing until the mayonnaise is nice and thick.
5. Store in a clean glass jar in the refrigerator for up to 5 days.

Tofu Mayonnaise

About 1-½ cups.

This mild-tasting creamy tofu mayonnaise works well on sandwiches or in mayonnaise-based potato and vegetable salads. You can easily reduce the fat content by substituting part of the oil with water or plain soy milk.

It's best to make this mayonnaise in a blender, so you have to do less scraping down the sides of the container.

Ingredients

1 12-ounce box soft silken tofu

¼ cup mild-flavored oil, such as canola or safflower

1 tablespoon lemon juice

1 tablespoon sugar

1-½ teaspoons prepared Dijon mustard

1 teaspoon white wine or apple cider vinegar

½ teaspoon salt

1. Combine all of the ingredients in a blender and beat until smooth and creamy.

2. Store in a clean glass jar in the refrigerator for up to 4 days.

Vegan Honey Mustard Spread

About 1-½ cups.

This spread is similar to the sweet mustard sandwich spread you buy in jars at the supermarket, though this version tastes fresher and not as cloyingly sweet.

Ingredients

   ½ cup plain full fat soy milk

   ½ teaspoon sea salt

   4 tablespoons Dijon mustard

   2 tablespoons honey

   1 tablespoon white wine or apple cider vinegar

   1 cup safflower, sunflower, or canola oil

1. Measure all the ingredients except the oil into blender, food processor with steel blade, or a Kitchen Aid mixer with a whip attachment.

2. Blend on medium speed (or turn on food processor) and gradually add the oil, drop by drop.

3. Once the mixture starts to thicken, add the oil a little faster in a trickle.

4. Keep mixing the spread until it's nice and thick. Store in a clean glass jar in the refrigerator for up to 5 days.

Soups

Nothing satisfies quite like soup. Good vegan soup is not difficult to make. The most important requirement is a flavorful stock.

Unfortunately, homemade stock is something most people don't bother to make (although you can make a lot of it at one time and freeze it). However, you can find many vegan stock alternatives, including vegetable and mushroom stock in cans, aseptic packages, and even powdered varieties.

Be sure to read the labels. Many natural food stores carry all kinds of "vegetarian" stocks, but that doesn't make them vegan. Often those fake chicken and beef stocks contain non-vegan ingredients, such as whey (a byproduct of cheese making) and lactose.

However, you can find 100% vegan broth powders, and we also have given you a recipe so you can make your own "chicken" flavored broth powder. Beef flavored stock is a little trickier. If you are lucky enough to have a natural foods store near you that sells a brand called Abco, it is excellent.

Our favorite all-purpose broth, that works in virtually any recipe, is a delicious broth cube called Morga. It's not inexpensive. But Morga cubes are the least salty, most fresh-tasting vegan broth you will ever taste (short of homemade). It's organic, and contains no MSG . All it has is the essence of flavorful vegetables.

Mock Chicken Broth Powder

About 2 cups.

Dissolve about 1-2 tablespoons per cup of hot water to make chicken flavored stock.

Ingredients

　　　1-⅓ cups nutritional yeast flakes

　　　2 tablespoons potato flour (do not substitute potato starch)

　　　3 tablespoons onion powder

　　　½ teaspoon garlic powder

　　　1 tablespoon sea salt

　　　2-½ teaspoons garlic granules or powder

　　　1 tablespoon vegan soymilk powder

　　　1 tablespoon sugar

　　　2 teaspoons poultry seasoning

　　　1 teaspoon paprika

　　　½ teaspoon turmeric

1.　Place all the ingredients in a blender and mix for 1-2 minutes.

2.　Store in an airtight container in a cool, dark place. (This mix keeps for a long time.)

Onion Soup

4 main dish servings.

This recipe is about as close as you'll get to real French Onion Soup. It makes a hearty broth full of deep flavors and mellow onions that practically melt in your mouth.

If you wish, float a round of sourdough or French bread on this soup, topped with a slice of vegan mozzarella. Microwave the soup on high for about 30 seconds to soften the cheese.

This soup makes a nice first course for a big dinner party, or a great late-night pick me up all by itself.

Ingredients

4-5 cups very thinly sliced onions (we like to use red onions, for their color and sweetness)

6 cups water

3 Morga broth cubes

2 tablespoons tamari

2 teaspoons sugar

3 cloves garlic, crushed

1. In a large soup pot, combine all the ingredients.
2. Bring to a boil, then reduce the heat and simmer very slowly (about 30-40 minutes) until the onions are falling apart.
3. Taste, and adjust the seasonings. Serve hot.

California Carrot Soup

About 4 main-dish bowls, or 6-8 smaller servings.

For this soup, there's about 10 minutes of peeling and chopping work, but after that it's just simmering and blending. An immersion blender makes this recipe go even more quickly.

You can make this soup ahead of time and refrigerate it for up to three days. Just make sure to heat it well before serving. If you want to try something fancy, you can swirl a teaspoon of vegan sour cream into each bowl right before serving.

In case you haven't used one before, an immersion blender is a device with a long handle and a small circular blade at the bottom. It's great tool to make your cooking life easier. You just put the wand in the soup, flip the switch, and blend right in the pot. The soup might not be quite as silky smooth as the kind you liquefy in the blender, but it's still good, and there's a lot less cleanup.

Ingredients

8 medium carrots, peeled and chopped

4 small potatoes, peeled and chopped

1 medium onion, chopped

1 tablespoon orange zest (grated orange peel)

1 juice of an orange

2 tablespoons olive oil

2 tablespoons brown sugar

1 tablespoon chopped garlic

1 teaspoon ginger root, peeled and chopped

5-8 fresh basil leaves

1. Heat the olive oil in a soup pot, and cook the onions over medium heat until they are translucent.

2. Add the carrots, and stir for 2 minutes.

3. Add the potatoes, and stir for 2 more minutes.

4. Add the orange zest, garlic, ginger, and basil. Cook on high heat for 5 minutes, stirring constantly so nothing sticks.

5. Add enough water to barely cover the vegetables, and simmer covered for about 30 minutes, or until the vegetables are soft.

6. Stir the orange juice and brown sugar into the mixture.

7. Puree in a blender or food processor until smooth, or use an immersion blender right in the pot. Add more a little more water if the soup is too thick.

8. Serve very hot.

Creamy Potato Soup

4 servings.

Potato soup is comfort food. This thick, smooth soup warms the belly and the soul. The perfect chaser would be some simple steamed green vegetables, like broccoli or green beans, dressed with a light sauce, like Sauteed Broccoli with Garlic and Lemon (page 90).

It's easy to double or triple this recipe for a party, and the soup keeps well in the fridge. Don't add the sour cream until the last minute, and make sure you don't let the soup boil when you reheat it.

You can also skip the potato mashing step. But we think the extra couple of minutes it takes is worth it since the result is so good.

If you don't like peeling potatoes, invest in a good quality vegetable peeler. Plus, instead of trying to delicately peel them, use a long hacking motion away from your body. You may waste a bit of the good part of the potato because it sticks to the skins, but you'll save a lot of time.

Ingredients

2 tablespoons olive oil

1 cup onion, chopped

2 large cloves garlic, minced

3 tablespoons all purpose flour

4 tablespoons broth powder dissolved in 4 cups boiling water

3 tablespoons vegan margarine

4 cups peeled, diced potatoes (about 3 large)

1 cup plain soy milk

¼ cup vegan sour cream

Salt and freshly ground black pepper to taste

½ cup chives, chopped

1. Heat the olive oil in a soup pot over medium heat.

2. Add the onions and garlic and sauté until very soft, about 8-10 minutes.

3. Lower the heat and add the flour, stirring until smooth. Cook at least 1 minute, stirring constantly to cook away the raw flour taste.

4. Add the potatoes, broth, and margarine. Bring to a boil, then cover and reduce the heat.

5. Simmer gently for about 20 minutes, stirring occasionally until the potatoes are nice and tender.

6. Transfer the mixture to a bowl and mash the potatoes until smooth, or use an immersion blender. (Don't use a food processor, or the potatoes will become gluey.)

7. Return the soup to the pot. Stir in the soy milk, and season to taste with salt and freshly ground black pepper.

8. Just before serving, heat the soup and whisk in the vegan sour cream at the last minute.

9. Serve, garnished with the chopped chives.

Charles Degrace's Three-Bean California Chili

This recipe is based on Susan's uncle Chuck's "secret" recipe. We have only made minor variations, keeping his original method intact. You slowly stew the vegetables and beans in a small amount of liquid, but after the first five minutes you can completely ignore it.

As written, the recipe makes a fairly mild chili. But you can be as daring as you like with the chili powder, or add whatever ground chilis you may have available.

Ingredients

2 tablespoons olive oil

1 green pepper, seeded and coarsely chopped

1 cup onion, chopped

2 cloves garlic, sliced

1 14.5-ounce can whole tomatoes, chopped, with their juice

1 cup dry red wine

4 teaspoons chili powder

1 teaspoon garlic powder

1 teaspoon cumin

1 teaspoon oregano

1 teaspoon basil

2 teaspoons sugar

1 teaspoon salt

½ teaspoons black pepper

1 15-ounce can black beans

1 15-ounce can red kidney beans

1 15-ounce can white northern or pinto beans

1. Heat the 2 tablespoons of olive oil in a soup pot, and add the green pepper, onion, and garlic. Cook on medium heat for at least 5 minutes, stirring often, so the vegetables begin to soften but do not brown or burn.

2. When the vegetables are ready, add the tomatoes and their juice, the red wine, chili powder, garlic powder, ground cumin, oregano, basil, sugar, salt, and pepper.

3. Drain and rinse the beans thoroughly, and add to the pot.

4. Bring to a boil, then reduce heat, and simmer partially covered for 30 to 40 minutes. Take a peek occasionally, to make sure there is enough liquid and nothing sticks to the bottom of the pan.

5. When ready, dish into deep bowls, and garnish with all your favorite traditional chili accompaniments, such as chopped onion, vegan sour cream, and shredded vegan cheese.

Quick Bean and Carrot Soup

Serves 2-4.

This recipe involves very little chopping, just the carrots and an onion. Mostly you just measure spices and open a can of beans.

This soup is fragrant and spicy. Serve it with a cold vegetable salad dressed with a little soy yogurt and lemon juice, and maybe a little chopped fresh parsley or mint.

Ingredients

3 cups water

1 Morga bouillon cube

1 15-ounce can navy beans

½ large onion, chopped

4 medium carrots, chopped

1 clove garlic, sliced (optional)

1 ½ cups frozen peas, carrots, corn (any or all)

1 teaspoon garlic powder

1 teaspoon garam masala (an Indian seasoning sold in most natural food stores and gourmet shops)

½ teaspoon fenugreek powder

¼ teaspoon crushed red pepper

½ teaspoon savory leaf

1 teaspoon tarragon leaf

1 teaspoon cumin seed

½ - 1 teaspoon salt

½ teaspoon coriander

2 tablespoons olive oil

1. Put the water, Morga cube, onion, and carrots into a pot.

2. Simmer for 5 minutes.

3. Add the beans, spices, frozen veggies, and oil.

4. Simmer for 10 minutes, or until the carrots and onion are soft. Serve piping hot.

Minestrone

Serves 6-8.

This old standby is filled with vegetables and just enough pasta to make the soup a meal.

If you have access to fresh, ripe tomatoes, they make a big difference in this dish. The next best thing would be canned whole organic tomatoes in juice. Chop them in course chunks, and include all the juice when you add them.

Ingredients

2 tablespoons extra virgin olive oil

1 cup onion, chopped

1 cup celery, chopped

1 cup carrot, diced fine

1 cup summer squash, sliced into ½ inch thick rounds

1 cup green or red pepper, seeded and chopped

4 cloves garlic, sliced thin

1 cup flat leaf parsley, chopped

10 cups water

1 Morga broth cube

1 tablespoon dried Italian Seasoning

1 tablespoon sea salt

1 15-ounce can chickpeas, preferably organic, drained and rinsed

3 cups fresh tomatoes, chopped (or 1 15-ounce can whole organic tomatoes, coarsely chopped)

1 15-ounce can red or white kidney beans, preferably organic, drained and rinsed

1 cup elbow macaroni or small shell pasta

1. In a large soup pot, heat the olive oil over medium heat. Add all the vegetables, including the garlic and parsley, and sauté gently until they begin to give off a little liquid (3-4 minutes).

2. Add the water, Morga cube, Italian Seasoning, and sea salt. Simmer for about 10 minutes, uncovered.

3. Add the beans, chickpeas, tomatoes, and macaroni, and cook about 10 minutes more, until the pasta is tender.

Springtime Soup

About 4 servings.

This recipe is so simple, you won't believe how good it is. This soup is best when you make it with fresh peas and asparagus in the spring. But you can make it any time of year with frozen veggies, and it will be almost as good.

Serve the soup with crusty bread, maybe with a little Blender Hummus (page 134) as a spread.

Ingredients

4 cups fresh or frozen green peas

1 medium onion, chopped fine

3 cups fresh or frozen asparagus, with the tough ends removed

1 large russet potato, peeled and sliced

4 cups water

2 tablespoons vegan chicken broth powder

2 tablespoons tamari

1 tablespoon dried tarragon (or 2 tablespoons fresh)

1. Put the vegetables, water, broth powder, and tamari in a soup pot. Bring to a boil, then simmer gently until the asparagus and potatoes are soft, about 15-20 minutes. Stir in the tarragon.

2. Cool the soup slightly, then puree in batches in a blender.

3. Serve warm or hot.

Creamy White Bean Stew

Serves 2.

It's surprising that such humble ingredients could be so delicious. Plus, you probably already have everything to make this dish in your pantry or fridge.

You will need some good bread to sop up the sauce. Or if you're feeling ambitious, you could serve this stew on top of plain white rice or pasta.

Ingredients

2 tablespoons vegan margarine

1 small onion, chopped

½ pound white mushrooms, sliced

2 teaspoons unbleached, all purpose flour

1 cup plain soy milk

1 15-ounce can white beans, preferably organic, drained and rinsed (such as great northern, navy, or butter beans)

1 clove garlic, minced fine

1 teaspoon sea salt

1 teaspoon crushed red pepper flakes

Pinch of nutmeg

1. Heat the margarine over medium heat in a large nonstick skillet. When it's melted, add the onions and mushrooms and cook for several minutes, until they begin to soften.

2. Add the flour and stir the mixture for about two minutes, to cook off the raw flour taste.

3. Add the soy milk, beans, garlic, salt, red pepper, and a pinch of nutmeg. Reduce the heat and simmer for about 8 minutes, until the sauce is slightly thick. (Do not boil.) Serve very hot.

Creamy Tomato and Potato Soup

About 4 servings.

This soup is really more like a stew. If you don't have celery, or the particular frozen veggies listed here, don't worry. You can try it with whatever you have left in the refrigerator or freezer. The main thing that makes it somewhat unusual is the salsa.

We always have salsa around because we buy Pace Picante salsa in the huge size. (James loves corn chips and salsa.) Although we specify "medium" that may be somewhat spicy for some people. You can adjust the spiciness factor by using a milder salsa.

Ingredients

2 tablespoons olive oil

1 onion, chopped

2 stalks celery, chopped

3 cloves garlic, chopped

4 cups water

4 tablespoons "beef" broth powder or two bouillon cubes

1 cup medium salsa

2 tomatoes

1 tablespoon basil

1 bay leaf

4 or 5 medium potatoes

1-½ cups frozen peas

1 cup soy milk

1 tablespoon cornstarch

1. Place oil in a large soup pot. Add onion, celery, garlic, and cook for about 5 minutes over medium heat.

2. Add water, bouillon, potatoes, salsa, tomatoes, basil, and bay leaf. Cook for 30 minutes until the potatoes are tender.

3. Add the frozen peas and cook for 5 minutes.

4. Place the milk and cornstarch in a small jar, cover, and shake to mix. Add the mixture into the soup and stir to thicken.

5. Add salt and pepper to taste and serve.

Corn & Potato Chowder

Serves 4.

This is a satisfying soup that goes together quickly. If you like a creamier soup, you can blend some or all of it in a blender. (Blending cooked potatoes is a great way to make a soup extra creamy!)

Ingredients

2 tablespoons canola oil

1 onion, chopped

3 cups water

3 medium potatoes, diced

2 Morga bouillon cubes

½ teaspoon sage

¼ teaspoon marjoram

½ teaspoon coriander

1 teaspoon salt

2 cups frozen corn

2 tablespoons olive oil

2 cups soy milk

2 tablespoons rice or oat flour

1. Add oil to an 8-quart pot and cook the onion until it is translucent (about 5 minutes).

2. Add water, Morga cubes, spices, and potatoes. Bring to boil. Lower heat and simmer for 20 minutes.

3. Add the corn and the olive oil and simmer 10 minutes more.

4. Mix together milk and flour in a small bowl or jar.

5. Stir the milk/flour mixture into the pot, and simmer gently until it thickens. (Do not allow it to boil rapidly or the milk may curdle.)

Tofu, Tempeh, Lentils, and Beans

These recipes emphasize plant-based proteins. In a sense, all of them are legume-based: tofu and tempeh are made from soybeans. Lentils are a member of the pea and bean family.

In some recipes, we are quite generous with the olive oil or nut butters (such as tahini, which is sesame paste). But remember that all these protein sources, even full-fat tofu, are relatively low in fat and calories compared with meat, cheese, or eggs. Plus most people find that plant-based proteins are easier to digest.

Many of these recipes call for tempeh, a dense, chewy, meaty-tasting soybean product. Steaming tempeh for 10 to 20 minutes softens it a little bit and allows the tempeh to absorb the flavors of spices more readily.

Many of these dishes are delicious and satisfying enough to serve to meat eaters. They provide as much (or more) protein than most greasy fast food lunches. And they are a whole lot better for you.

Chicken Fried Tofu Cutlets

Serves 2 hungry vegans.

When you need a hot, filling comfort meal that really hits the spot, make these cutlets the centerpiece. This recipe probably requires the most work of any in this book. (You actually have to stand by the stove for about 5-10 minutes!) But since the technique is really easy, and the rewards are so great, we decided to include it in this book.

If you don't remember to press and drain the tofu ahead of time, the dish is still good. The coating may not be quite as crisp, and you might have better luck flipping the cutlets if you cut them into smaller squares. But if you remember to prep the tofu early in the day, you end up with crispier, crunchier cutlets at dinnertime.

Because the cutlets are thin, the frying takes almost no time. It takes just a few minutes per batch. Serve them with a fuss-free, kick-back-and-relax side dish like Mustard Roasted Potatoes (page 44), some frozen or canned sweet corn or Cupboard Three Bean Salad (page 92), and your favorite barbeque sauce.

You could also make a double batch of these cutlets and refrigerate the leftovers to make a Vegan Club Sandwich (page 120). The cutlets keep two to three days if you wrap them tightly in plastic wrap or foil.

Ingredients

    1 package extra firm tofu (water packed)

    1 cup unbleached all-purpose flour

    2 tablespoons poultry seasoning (or 1 tablespoons sage, 1 teaspoon thyme, 1 teaspoon marjoram, and 1 teaspoon black pepper)

    2-4 tablespoons canola or safflower oil for frying

1. Early in the day, drain and press the tofu. To press it, slice the slab in half. Lay both pieces side by side on a large shallow plate or a baking pan. Place a smaller plate on top of each piece, and rest a can of vegetables on each. Refrigerate.

2. About 10 minutes before you want to eat, remove the tofu from the fridge, remove the cans and plates, pour off the water, and slice the tofu into ½-inch thick slices. Set them aside in a single layer.

3. Mix the flour and poultry seasoning in a shallow bowl.

4. Pour about about 2-4 tablespoons of oil in a non-stick skillet over medium high heat until it's hot, but not smoking.

5. Dredge each slice of tofu in the flour, pressing the flour gently into the tofu. Lay as many pieces as will fit comfortably in a single layer in the pan.

6. Cook about 2 minutes, flip and cook two minutes more. Some of the coating will dislodge and leave blackened bits in the pan. Don't worry, they won't affect the flavor.

7. Drain the cutlets on paper towels. These are best eaten immediately, but also surprisingly good reheated in the toaster oven the next day.

Meet Loaf

Serves 6.

If you miss comfort foods like meat loaf with mashed potatoes and gravy, take heart. This easy recipe makes a big, hearty, tasty loaf that's so good, you won't worry about serving it to non-vegan guests. (Hence the bad pun "Meet Loaf.")

The secret ingredient that makes this loaf so tasty is a 100% vegan concoction called Bragg's Liquid Aminos. It's often found in the spice or sauces section of the supermarket.

Braggs adds a somewhat unique flavor to foods. You can use it in soups and sauces or with TVP and tofu. But you need to be careful when you use it. Because of its saltiness, you can easily add too much and make a dish completely unpalatable.

This hearty Meet Loaf sports the traditional ketchup topping. But you can also skip the ketchup, and make Real Gravy (page 12). And don't forget the mashed potatoes (page 53)!

If you happen to have any leftover Meet Loaf, it also makes terrific sandwiches.

Ingredients

  1 package firm tofu, drained and mashed

  ¾ cup wheat germ

  ¼ cup fresh flat leaf parsley, chopped (or 2 tablespoons dried parsley)

  ½ cup onion, finely diced

  2 tablespoons tamari or soy sauce

  3 tablespoons Bragg's Liquid Aminos

  1 tablespoon Dijon mustard

  1 clove garlic, minced (or 1 teaspoon granulated garlic)

  ½ teaspoon dried thyme

  1 teaspoon black pepper (not freshly ground, the powdery stuff)

  1 cup ketchup

1. Preheat the oven to 350 degrees.

2. Take all the ingredients except the ketchup, dump them into a big bowl, and mash them all together until they are thoroughly mixed.

3. Oil a standard loaf pan, then gently press the tofu mixture into it.

4. Bake uncovered for about 45 minutes.

5. Remove the loaf from the oven, and spread the ketchup over the top of the loaf.

6. Bake another 10-15 minutes, watching so the ketchup doesn't burn.

7. Let stand about 10 minutes before slicing.

Vegan Burgers

4 4-inch burgers (roughly "quarter pounder" size)

These burgers are much more economical than many packaged "veggie burgers." Make a double batch of these, cook them all, and wrap and freeze the leftovers. They are also 100% vegan, unlike many commercial versions.

The best thing is these burgers taste great! Of course, you can serve them on a toasted whole grain bun with all the traditional fixings: ketchup, mustard, relish, lettuce, tomato, pickle, and vegan mayonnaise. Or you can be a little more creative, and smother them with sautéed mushrooms, fried onions, and Real Gravy (page 12).

Either way, there's a lot to love about this burger substitute. It's easy to throw together, full of protein, low in fat, and best of all, it has no weird ingredients!

Ingredients

1 package firm tofu (water packed), drained

¼ cup wheat germ

¼-½ cup whole wheat pastry flour

1 tablespoon Bragg's Liquid Aminos

1 tablespoon nutritional yeast (optional)

½ teaspoon vegan bacon bits

2 tablespoon grated onion

¼ teaspoon garlic powder

1 teaspoon powdered vegan broth powder (vegetable, beef, or even chicken flavor)

½ teaspoon ground black pepper

¼ teaspoon salt

Sliced vegan cheese (optional)

1. Mash all the ingredients in a large bowl. Start with the smaller amount of flour, and use more only if you need it to hold the mixture together. You may want to use your hands to mix it completely. It's important that everything be thoroughly mashed together, so it forms a crumbly paste.

2. Heat about a tablespoon of bland oil (such as canola) in a non-stick skillet over medium heat.

3. Form the mixture into roughly 4-inch burgers, then sauté them slowly. Gently brown the burgers on one side, then the other. Cooking them on Medium heat (or even a little lower) with a longer cooking time is better than flash frying them because you want to cook away the raw flour taste. Cooking about 5 minutes per side is good, as long as you adjust the heat so they don't burn.

4. While the burgers cook, warm some nice whole grain or sprouted buns in a toaster oven and get all your favorite condiments ready. If you want vegan cheeseburgers, lay the vegan cheese slices on the buns while they're warming up. (Note: vegan cheese doesn't really melt, but it will soften.)

5. Put the burgers on the warmed buns, slather on your favorite fixings, and serve.

Easy Basmati Spinach Ragout

Serves 2-4.

This recipe is on the "make anytime" list. In other words, it's high on our list of favorite dinners.

This ragout is an adaptation of a much more complicated recipe. You can find the original in a cookbook called *Vegetarian Planet* by Didi Emmons. This great cookbook is filled with wonderful recipes and ideas (although they aren't necessarily easy or vegan).

Don't worry about the long list of ingredients. It's mostly spices. Basically, you chuck everything in a pot, and it cooks itself.

Ingredients

1 tablespoon canola oil

1-½ teaspoon ground coriander

1 teaspoon ground mustard

1 teaspoon ground cumin

½ teaspoon black pepper

1 teaspoon ground ginger

½ teaspoon cayenne pepper

1 14-ounce can of coconut milk (don't use "light" coconut milk)

4 cups water

1 cup basmati rice

1 16-ounce package of firm tofu

2 carrots, peeled and sliced into half rounds

1 10-ounce package frozen spinach

Salt and pepper to taste

1. In a large pot, heat the oil and add the spices. Cook the spices for a few minutes until they are fragrant.

2. Add the water and coconut milk, and bring to a gentle boil. (Be careful not to let this boil over or you'll have a big mess!)

3. Add the basmati rice and tofu. Reduce the heat to a simmer (use the same temperature you would use to cook rice). Cook for about 10 minutes.

4. Add the carrots and cook for 10 minutes more.

5. Defrost the spinach in the microwave, and squeeze out the extra water.

6. After 20 minutes of cooking the rice should look more or less done. (If not, cook for a while longer.)

7. When the rice is done, add the spinach. Cook for another 3-5 minutes to heat up the spinach.

8. Take the stew off the heat, and let it sit for 5 minutes. Then add salt and pepper to taste, and dig in!

Tempeh Stroganoff

4 generous main dish servings.

This recipe takes its spicing inspiration from an old (handwritten!) cookbook called *Cooking with Tempeh* by Clare Seguin that we found at a used book store. The technique is simple – you steam the tempeh, sauté it with some veggies, add a little vegan sour cream, and you're good to go.

Not all vegans are mushroom fans, so we added the peppers and peas. In our case, James eats all the 'shrooms - and Susan has plenty of other veggies. Traditionalists and mushroom lovers can opt not to include these non-stroganoff type items, but these optional ingredients do add a lot to the flavor of the dish.

Ingredients

1 package of tempeh

1 package of wide noodles (such as "No Yolks" dumpling noodles)

2 tablespoon oil

¼ cup tamari sauce

1 tablespoon ground cumin

2 teaspoons black pepper

2 tablespoon red wine vinegar, wine, or apple cider vinegar

½ pound fresh sliced mushrooms (or more)

1 green or red pepper, chopped (optional)

1 cup peas (optional)

½-1 cup soy sour cream

1. Put a pot of water on to boil and cook the noodles according to package directions. When the noodles are done, drain them, and put them back in the pot. Set aside.

2. Steam the tempeh for 20 minutes.

3. While the tempeh steams, put the oil, tamari, wine, cumin, pepper, and mushrooms in a large pan on medium heat. Cook until the mushrooms are browned.

4. After the tempeh is done steaming, cut it into cubes, and add it to the mushroom pan. Add the optional veggies if you are using them, and cook for 5 minutes or so.

5. Turn the heat off the mushroom mix, remove from the burner, and stir in the sour cream.

6. Pour the mushroom sour cream sauce in the pot with the noodles, stir, and serve.

Brown Lentils with Sun-Dried Tomato Vinaigrette

Serves 4.

This warm, hearty, incredibly delicious dish is made from ordinary brown lentils. Serve them on a bed of steamed spinach for a special treat.

Ingredients

  2 cups dried brown lentils, rinsed and carefully picked over (watch out for small stones)

  1 bay leaf

  1 medium onion, peeled and chopped

  2 cloves garlic, minced

  4 tablespoons extra virgin olive oil

  2 tablespoons white wine vinegar

  2 tablespoons sun-dried tomatoes packed in oil, drained and minced fine

  1 tablespoon oil from sun-dried tomatoes

  2 teaspoons dried marjoram

1. Put the lentils in a pot and cover with water. Add the bay leaf and the onion. Bring to a boil, and cook until the lentils are tender, about 20 minutes. Discard the bay leaf.

2. Whisk the garlic, oil, vinegar, sun-dried tomatoes, tomato oil, and marjoram in a small bowl.

3. Drain the lentils. Add the dressing while they are still warm, and serve warm or at room temperature.

Barbecued Tempeh

2 main dish servings.

This dish is one of the easiest and best ways to prepare tempeh. Tempeh is not only high in protein, its texture holds up beautifully in situations where tofu would just disintegrate.

You could serve barbecued tempeh as a delicious (if messy) sandwich in split toasted whole grain buns. We also like to use it in "roll ups" where we just put the mix in a tortilla with a little lettuce or sprouts. To make a meal out of it, try serving roll ups alongside Cupboard Three Bean Salad (page 92), or serve plain barbecued tempeh along with some Vegan Mashed Potatoes (page 53).

Ingredients

   8 ounces tempeh, defrosted

   1 large onion, halved and sliced very thin

   2 cups of your favorite barbeque sauce

1. Preheat oven to 350 degrees.

2. Cut the tempeh into ½-inch cubes. Put the tempeh, onions, and barbecue sauce into a casserole dish.

3. Cover the casserole, and bake for about 30 minutes.

Slow Roasted Tofu

Serves 2-3.

This method of making tofu involves oven-braising it in a highly seasoned liquid, so it absorbs as much flavor as possible. You end up with firm, tasty tofu that can be served hot or cold. It can stand in for chicken or meat in some traditional dishes.

Ingredients

1 package extra firm, water-packed tofu, drained and sliced into ½ inch thick slices

1 cup boiling water

2 tablespoons vegan vegetable, chicken, or beef-flavored broth powder

2 tablespoons tamari

2 tablespoons wine

3 tablespoons tahini

1 tablespoon miso

2 teaspoons olive oil

2 teaspoons spices (optional). For flavor variations try Chinese Five spice, ginger, garlic granules, or taco seasoning.

1. Preheat the oven to 375 degrees. Arrange the tofu in a single layer in a large baking pan with high sides.

2. Dissolve the broth powder in the water.

3. In a small bowl or glass jar, mix the tamari, wine, tahini, miso, and olive oil. Combine with the broth and pour over the tofu.

3. Cover the pan tightly with aluminum foil. Bake covered for 15 minutes, until the liquid is simmering.

4. Uncover and continue to bake another 15-20 minutes, until the liquid is almost completely absorbed. Baste the tofu with the olive oil and bake until the pan is almost dry and the tofu is firm.

Greek Tofu

2 generous servings.

Lemon, oregano, garlic, olive oil, and white wine turn tofu into a dish worthy of company. Be generous with the lemon juice, and be sure to add the small amount of sugar. That little bit of sweetness helps blend all the flavors together.

Preground black pepper is also essential for optimal flavor. For a complete meal, serve this dish with steamed fresh spinach, Broccoli Tomato Salad (page 87), and Middle Eastern Rice Pilaf (page 68).

Ingredients

- 1 package extra firm tofu (water packed), drained and pressed to remove as much water as possible
- 4 tablespoons extra virgin olive oil, divided
- Juice of 1 lemon
- 1 teaspoon sugar
- 3 cloves garlic, minced
- 3 teaspoons dried Greek oregano
- ½ cup dry white wine
- ¼ teaspoon ground black pepper

1. Heat 2 tablespoons olive oil in a large nonstick skillet over medium heat. Dry the tofu well on paper towels, and when the oil is hot add the slices to the skillet in a single layer. Turn up the heat so the oil stays quite hot but does not smoke. When the tofu is brown on one side, flip it over and brown the other.

2. Reduce the heat, and add the remaining oil and other ingredients. Bring to a gentle simmer, and cook uncovered until the liquid has reduced by about half. Serve hot.

Vegan Enchilada Casserole

Serves 4-6

This is a great potluck or party dish. The hardest part is the assembly, which is not exactly rocket science. After that, the casserole slowly bakes. You can make this dish ahead of time, cool and refrigerate it, and serve it reheated the next day. It's just as good, maybe even a little better as a leftover. The avocado garnish is optional, but extremely delicious, so include it if you can get a good ripe avocado.

Some people like to put refried beans into vegan enchiladas, but we prefer them on the side, along with some rice cooked in half vegetable stock, half tomato juice.

If you make this casserole for a dinner party, you might serve a simple dessert of vegan vanilla ice cream drizzled with honey, and sprinkled with toasted pecans and a little cinnamon. Yum!

Ingredients

2 tablespoons olive oil

1 small white onion, chopped

1 green bell pepper, seeded and chopped

1 red bell pepper, seeded and chopped

1 jalapeno pepper, seeded and minced

1 package firm tofu, water packed, drained and crumbled

1 small can chopped ripe black olives

2 cans commercial mild red enchilada sauce

2 cans tomatoes and green chilis

¼ cup vegan chicken broth powder

1 dozen yellow corn tortillas

1 large ripe avocado, peeled, pitted, and cubed, for serving (optional)

1. Preheat the oven to 350 degrees. Spray a 9 x 13 baking pan with nonstick canola oil spray.

2. Heat the olive oil in a nonstick skillet over medium heat. Add the onion and peppers and sauté for about 10 minutes, stirring occasionally, until soft.

3. Add the onion-pepper mixture to the tofu, along with the black olives. Mix until combined.

4. Empty the cans of enchilada sauce and tomato-chilis into a large microwave-safe mixing bowl. Whisk in the broth powder, and heat in the microwave on high for about 2 minutes until it is bubbling. Whisk again, and set aside.

5. Line the bottom of the baking pan with half the corn tortillas, tearing them to fit into the empty spots. Spread all of the tofu mixture on them. Then top with the other half of the corn tortillas.

6. Pour all the sauce over the casserole. Cover with foil, and bake for about 45 minutes, until hot and bubbling.

7. Right before serving, sprinkle with a cubed avocado.

Tofu Scramble

2 generous servings.

Fantastic Foods makes what is essentially a prepared spice package that you add to tofu to make a "scrambler." It works well, but sometimes you don't have it available. So this recipe is our version of scrambled tofu for those special weekends when you want a big hearty breakfast. We like to serve it with buttered English muffins.

Ingredients

½ block firm tofu, broken into small chunks and marinated in 2 tablespoons lemon juice

½ block firm tofu, mashed

½ teaspoon turmeric

½ teaspoon ground mustard seed

¼ cup water

1 teaspoon tahini

2 tablespoons oil

1 cup scallions, chopped

3 garlic cloves, sliced or diced

1 teaspoon mustard (stone ground)

2 tablespoons nutritional yeast

½ cup fresh tomato, chopped

2 tablespoons fresh basil, coarsely chopped

1. Cut tofu block in half. Break one half into small chunks. Place in small bowl and marinate in lemon juice. Mash the other half with a fork or potato masher and set aside.

2. Mix turmeric and mustard seed into mashed tofu.

3. Make a tahini sauce by placing the tahini and the ¼ cup water in a small jar. Cover and shake vigorously to dissolve the tahini.

4. Place the oil in pan and heat over medium heat. Add scallions and garlic and cook until they have have softened a bit.

5. Lower heat to medium low and add mashed tofu mix. Stir and cook until it turns yellow (from the turmeric).

6. Add the mustard, nutritional yeast, and tahini mixture. Stir and cook until it thickens.

7. Add marinated tofu, basil, and tomatoes. Cook until tomatoes are heated.

Hoppin' James

Serves 4.

We make this dish on New Year's Eve or New Year's Day, since we can never seem to remember which day you're supposed to make it to get all that good luck. Sometimes we make it December 31, and have leftovers on January 1, so we are definitely covered in the luck department. It's a yummy way to start off the year!

Ingredients

1 15-ounce can of black-eyed peas (frozen or fresh are okay too)

1 box long grain and wild rice

2 tablespoons oil

4 large garlic cloves, slices

2 carrots, chopped

1 onion, chopped

1 green bell pepper, chopped

¼ teaspoon paprika

½ teaspoon cumin

¼ teaspoon ground fennel

¼ teaspoon thyme

¼ teaspoon marjoram

⅛ teaspoon cayenne (if desired)

1. Rinse, drain, and if necessary defrost the black-eyed peas.

2. Cook the rice according to package directions.

3. Chop the veggies. Place the oil in a saucepan, heat over medium heat, and add the onion.

4. Cook the onion and when it is starting to become translucent, add other veggies and spices. Cook the veggies until tender.

5. Once veggies are cooked, add the beans and cook for a few minutes to warm them up.

6. Mix the bean/veggie mixture with the cooked rice and serve.

Red Lentil Stew

Serves 4.

We often refer to lentils as "hearty food." This stew is satisfying when it's cold outside and you want something filling and tasty. Although it looks like a lot of ingredients, they are mostly spices. Once everything is in the pot, you can pretty much ignore it.

Ingredients

  1 cup red lentils

  3-½ cups water

  1 bouillon cube

  2 stalks celery, chopped

  3 medium carrots, grated

  1 small crown broccoli, chopped

  2 tablespoons olive oil

  ½ teaspoon salt

  ½ teaspoon garlic granules

  ¼ teaspoon crushed red pepper

  ½ teaspoon onion granules

  ½ teaspoon sage

  ¼ teaspoon marjoram

  ¼ teaspoon sugar

1. Chop the veggies.Put the water, oil, bouillon, and spices in a pot and bring to a boil.

2. Add the lentils and simmer for 10 minutes uncovered over medium heat.

3. Add the vegetables and simmer 10 more minutes uncovered. Serve plain or over rice.

Stella Blues Breakfast

Serves 2.

While on the island of Maui in Hawaii, we found a wonderful restaurant called Stella Blues Cafe. This recipe was inspired by the mouth-watering breakfast we enjoyed there one morning. If you are ever in the area, be sure to include a Stella Blues meal in your plans.

Ingredients

   1 pound firm tofu, cubed

   ½ green pepper, chopped

   ½ red pepper, chopped

   1 teaspoon garlic powder

   1 teaspoon stone-ground mustard

   1 teaspoon ground coriander

   1 teaspoon tarragon

   1 tablespoon tahini

   ½ onion, chopped

   1 tomato, chopped

   ¼ cup water

   2 tablespoons olive oil

1. Sauté the onion in olive oil until it starts to become translucent.

2. Put tahini, water, and mustard in a small jar. Shake until tahini dissolves (hold the jar up to check the size of the chunks that drift to the bottom).

3. Add tahini mix, tofu, and spices to the onion. Cook for a few minutes to release flavors and reduce the liquid somewhat.

4. Add red and green pepper to the mixture. Cook until the pepper starts to become tender. Stir in the tomato just before serving.

Desserts

I f you have a sweet tooth, you need to rise to the challenge of developing vegan desserts that still satisfy, even without butter or eggs. In this book, we have included our favorite *easy* vegan desserts.

Although we love making pies, you won't find any of them here because they require making separate crusts and careful baking. Instead, you'll find things like mousse, cakes, bars, and simple fruit desserts. These recipes don't require any sort of preparation beyond measuring, mixing, and cooking!

Over the years, we've come to realize that the "time saving" you gain from using a baking mix is really negligible. It takes maybe two extra minutes to measure out those ingredients you get in the box (flour, sugar and so forth). But when you bake something from scratch, you don't get all the creepy chemicals and nasty hydrogenated oils that are included in most baking mixes. You actually *know* what's in your baked goods because you put it there.

One final note about vegan baked goods. It's best to get them into the oven as fast as possible because they don't have eggs in them to help emulsify the ingredients and trap air during the baking process. Once your cake or bars have cooled, wrap them tightly and store them in the refrigerator to keep them light and moist.

Nutty Brownies

Makes 9.

These brownies are chocolaty, rich, and nutty, but not overly sweet. Ideally, try to use the best-quality dutch process cocoa you can find, but of course, Hershey's works too!

Use a light touch when mixing the cocoa mixture to the flour. If you mix too much, you can start to toughen the gluten in the flour, and your brownies won't be dense and moist. Try using a big flexible spatula to gently fold the chocolate mixture into the dry ingredients, and don't worry about a few little lumps.

We love big walnut chunks in our brownies, but you can also use pecans, unsalted cashews, macadamia nuts, or even unsalted peanuts.

Ingredients

6 ounces firm silken tofu (half a block)

2 teaspoons egg replacer

1 cup sugar

½ cup mildly flavored oil (such as canola or safflower)

1 teaspoon pure vanilla extract

½ cup cocoa powder

¾ cup water

1-¾ cups unbleached all-purpose flour

¾ teaspoon baking soda

1 teaspoon non-alumnium baking powder

¾ cup walnut chunks

1. Preheat the oven to 350 degrees. Oil an 8 or 9-inch square baking pan. Measure the tofu, honey, oil, vanilla, cocoa, egg replacer, and water into a blender, mixer, or a food processor with a steel blade. Blend or process the mixture until it is nice and creamy, scraping down the sides of the container occasionally.

2. In a large mixing bowl, stir the flour, baking soda, and baking powder together with a fork.

3. Add the wet ingredients to the dry, and gently fold them together until there are no white streaks of flour. Do not over-mix, or your brownies will be dry.

4. Fold the walnuts in quickly. Spread the batter into the oiled square pan and bake for 30-35 minutes. Allow the brownies to cool completely before cutting them into squares.

Vegan Orange-Spice Cake

This slightly sweet, subtly spiced cake requires nothing more than a sprinkling of powdered sugar to finish it off. However, since this cake is delicious enough to be a spectacular ending for a dinner party, you can go all out by icing it with Vegan Chocolate Icing (page 186) or Easy Vegan Cake Glaze (page 187).

This wonderful cake is also one that even a kitchen novice can make successfully. In fact, measuring the ingredients takes more time than actually mixing the cake.

Ingredients

1-½ cups sifted unbleached all purpose flour

¾ cup sugar

1 teaspoon baking powder

½ teaspoon salt

1 teaspoon nutmeg

½ teaspoon cinnamon

½ teaspoon allspice

1 cup orange juice (freshly squeezed is best, but the stuff from a carton is okay too)

½ cup mildly flavored vegetable oil, such as canola or safflower

1 tablespoon grated orange zest

1 tablespoon apple cider vinegar

1 teaspoon pure vanilla extract

1. Preheat the oven to 350 degrees. Mix the flour, sugar, baking soda, salt, and spices with a whisk in a large mixing bowl.

2. In another bowl, whisk together the orange juice, oil, orange zest vinegar, and vanilla.

3. Fold the juice mixture into the dry ingredients, stirring gently until the batter is smooth.

4. Grease and flour an 8-inch round cake pan. Pour in the batter, and spread it out evenly.

5. Bake about 30 minutes, or until a toothpick inserted in the center comes out clean. Let the cake cool in the pan about 10 minutes before removing it from the pan. Let the cake cool thoroughly on a wire rack before icing or glazing.

Vegan Chocolate Icing

Enough to ice one Vegan Orange-Spice Cake.

This smooth icing is enhanced with a little liqueur, and it's super-easy to make. You may substitute almost any sweet spirit for the Grand Marnier. You might try Chambord, Frangelico, or Drambuie.

Ingredients

½ cup vegan chocolate chips or chopped bittersweet chocolate

3 tablespoons vegan margarine

1 tablespoon honey

1 tablespoon Grand Marnier

1. Place the chocolate and margarine in a heavy, microwave safe bowl that holds at least 20 ounces.

2. Microwave the chocolate and margarine on high for 30 seconds. Check it to see if the chocolate has started to melt. If not, cook on high for another 15-30 seconds. (Be careful, the bowl may get hot!)

3. Once the chocolate-margarine mixture has melted, whisk it vigorously with a small wire whisk. Then whisk in the honey and liqueur until it is smooth.

4. Wait until the icing has cooled completely and only use on a completely cooled cake. Once you've iced the cake, store it in the refrigerator.

Easy Vegan Cake Glaze

Enough to lightly glaze one Vegan Orange-Spice Cake.

This recipe has just two ingredients, and the only skills you need are the ability to measure and stir!

If you double the recipe, you also can use it on Lemon Blueberry Cake (page 190).

Ingredients

    1 cup confectioner's sugar

    1-2 tablespoons fresh lemon or orange juice

1. Measure the sugar into a mixing bowl.

2. Add the juice, and stir with a fork or spoon until you get a perfectly smooth glaze.

3. Pour or drizzle on top of a completely cooled cake.

Applesauce Cake

About 10 slices.

For this recipe, you just mix the dry ingredients, mix the wet ingredients, combine, and bake. The cake is easy, very low in fat, and delicious. You don't have to use the nuts, but they do add something special to this cake.

You can glaze this with Easy Vegan Cake Glaze (page 187), or just dust it with a little powdered sugar. For a special occasion, serve it with vegan ice cream.

Ingredients

1 cup unsweetened applesauce

3 teaspoons egg replacer, blended with 4 tablespoons water

2 teaspoons pure vanilla extract

1 cup soy milk

1 cup plus 2 tablespoons sugar

2-½ cups whole wheat pastry flour

2 teaspoons cinnamon

1-½ teaspoons baking soda

1-½ teaspoons baking powder

1. Preheat the oven to 325 degrees. Spray a nonstick bundt pan with canola oil spray.

2. In a large mixing bowl, combine the flour, sugar, baking soda, and baking powder.

3. In a blender or food processor, blend the applesauce, egg replacer, vanilla extract, and soy milk.

4. Gently stir the wet ingredients into the dry, mixing just until moistened. Don't overmix, or your cake will be tough and dry.

5. Pour the batter into the bundt pan, and bake 50-60 minutes, until a toothpick inserted in the cake comes out clean. Cool about 10 minutes before removing from the pan. Allow the cake to cool completely on a wire rack.

Lemon Blueberry Cake

About 10-12 slices.

This easy recipe makes an incredibly moist cake. Just be sure to put the cake in the oven immediately after mixing. Non-vegan cakes contain eggs, which help trap air bubbles in the batter as it rises. Vegan batters are a little more delicate, so it's best to mix them and get them in the oven quickly.

Bake this cake in a tube pan (often also called an angel food cake pan). You can dust it with confectioners sugar, or top it with Easy Vegan Cake Glaze (page 187).

Ingredients

6 ounces soft silken tofu (½ block)

2 teaspoons egg replacer

¾ cup water

½ cup freshly squeezed lemon juice

2 teaspoons grated lemon rind

½ cup mildly flavored oil, like canola or safflower

2-½ cups unbleached all purpose flour

1 cup sugar

1 ½ teaspoons baking powder

1 teaspoon nutmeg

½ teaspoon salt

1-½ cups blueberries, fresh or frozen

1. Preheat the oven to 350 degrees. Oil a bundt or tube pan and have it ready.

2. Put the tofu, water, egg replacer, lemon juice, oil, and lemon zest into a food processor with a steel blade, and process until smooth.

3. In another bowl, mix the flour, sugar, baking soda, nutmeg, and salt until combined.

4. Fold the flour mixture into the tofu mixture. Stir until combined, but to not overmix or the cake may be tough and dry.

5. Fold in the blueberries, then pour the batter into the pan and place it in the oven immediately.

6. Bake 45-50 minutes, until a toothpick inserted into the cake comes out clean.

7. Cool in the pan about 10 minutes. Then remove and cool on a wire rack.

8. Move the cake to a serving plate, and dust with confectioner's sugar or drizzle with glaze.

Vegan Double Chocolate Cake

Variations of this simple chocolate cake have been around for years. It's easy to make and enhanced with the addition of chopped chocolate. You could leave the extra chocolate out if you wish. It's easy to vary the flavor of this cake by adding ½ cup chopped nuts (walnuts or pecans are good), a tablespoon of flavored liqueur (try Amaretto, Frangelico, or Grand Marnier), or some chopped dried cherries or cranberries.

For a special occasion, you can double the recipe to make two 9-inch layers. Then fill and frost the cake with a triple batch of Vegan Chocolate Icing (page 186).

Ingredients

1-½ cups unbleached all purpose flour

1 cup sugar

¼ cup dutch processed cocoa powder

1 teaspoon baking soda

½ teaspoon salt

⅓ cup mildly flavored vegetable oil, such as canola or safflower

1 teaspoon pure vanilla extract

1 teaspoon distilled white vinegar or apple cider vinegar

1 cup water

½ cup chopped vegan semi-sweet chocolate or vegan chocolate chips

1. Preheat the oven to 350 degrees. Spray an 8 x 8 square or a 9-inch round cake pan with canola oil cooking spray.

2. Sift together the flour, sugar, cocoa, baking soda, and salt into a large bowl. Add the oil, vanilla, vinegar, and water. Gently mix until smooth.

3. Pour into the prepared pan, and bake for 35-45 minutes, until a toothpick inserted into the cake comes out clean. Allow to cool at least 10 minutes before removing from the pan. Cool completely before frosting.

Low Fat Apple Crisp

8-10 servings.

This recipe is a good dessert to make for a crowd. Aside from peeling and slicing apples, it's a mix and bake dish.

This apple crisp is not only delicious, it contains a minimum of fat. Serve this with your favorite vegan vanilla ice cream.

Ingredients

8 cups tart/sweet apples, such as Braeburn or Macintosh, peeled and thinly sliced

½-¾ cup sugar

1-½ teaspoons ground cinnamon

2 tablespoons corn starch

1 teaspoon nutmeg

¼ teaspoon sea salt

2 cups (or a little more) low-fat vegan granola of your choice

½ cup chopped toasted pecans

3 tablespoons melted vegan margarine

1. Preheat the oven to 375 degrees. Spray a 13 x 9 rectangular pan with canola oil cooking spray.

2. In a big bowl, combine the apples, sugar, cornstarch, spices, and salt. Mix well. Add the apple mixture to the pan.

3. Put the granola and nuts into a blender, and turn on for just a few seconds, to break up the granola chunks. Sprinkle over the apples. Drizzle with the melted margarine. Bake for about 40 minutes, or until the apples are tender and bubbling.

Easy Berry Sauce

2-3 servings.

Make this sauce when fresh berries are at their peak. You can use all strawberries, all blueberries, or a combination of raspberries, blackberries, and blueberries. Of course, here in Northern Idaho, we have local huckleberries that make a wonderful sauce!

Drizzle this sauce on vanilla or chocolate vegan ice cream. You can also use this as a luscious topping for Vegan Pancakes or Waffles (page 42), or even fresh-from-the-oven Vegan Biscuits (page 26).

Ingredients

   3 cups fresh berries (strawberries, blueberries, raspberries, or blackberries)

   ½ cup mild honey (such as clover honey) or sugar

   1 tablespoon vegan margarine

   1-2 tablespoons liqueur (try Grand Marnier with strawberries or blueberries, or Amaretto with raspberries and blackberries)

1. Wash and stem the berries. If you are using strawberries, cut them in halves or quarters.

2. Place the berries in a large nonstick skillet, add the honey and margarine, and heat very gently, stirring and gently crushing until the berries begin to give off some juice.

3. When the mixture is nice and warm, pour it over ice cream, pancakes, or biscuits.

Chocolate Bananas Foster

4 generous servings.

Even if you don't like bananas, this recipe includes another great topping for ice cream or pancakes. It takes almost no effort for a spectacular result!

The recipe calls for a generous amount of margarine, and you could reduce it a bit. But it's really necessary to create a rich, slightly butterscotch-flavored sauce. After all, it *is* dessert.

Ingredients

   5 tablespoons vegan margarine

   ¼ cup raw sugar, date sugar, or brown sugar

   ½ cup chopped pecans

   1 teaspoon Brandy or Grand Marnier (optional)

   ½ cup shaved vegan semi-sweet chocolate

   4 ripe bananas, peeled, sliced in half lengthwise, and sprinkled with a little lemon juice

1. Heat the margarine in a large nonstick skillet on medium low heat, just until it is melted. (Don't let it sizzle.) Add the sugar, and stir until the sugar has melted into the sauce.

2. Lay the bananas in a single layer in the skillet, and baste them with the butter sauce until they are quite hot.

3. Stir in the liqueur (if using). Place in serving dish and sprinkle the chocolate over the bananas. Serve right away.

Vegan Chocolate Mousse

About 4 cups.

This recipe is more like a pudding than a mousse, since of course, it has no eggs. But it's so good, no one will know it's made with tofu. It does include quite a bit of oil, and you could eliminate some of it if you're worried about the fat content. However, the pudding really does need some fat to give it a smooth, creamy consistency. Plus once you split it up into 4-6 servings, it's really not so bad, especially for a dessert.

Ingredients

> 12 ounces soft tofu (not silken)
>
> ¼ cup bland oil, such as canola or safflower
>
> 1 cup sugar (or a little more)
>
> ⅓ cup cocoa
>
> 1 ½ teaspoons pure vanilla extract
>
> ¼ teaspoon salt

1. Measure everything into a blender, and blend until very smooth, scraping down the sides of the blender periodically.
2. Chill at least 2 hours, until firm.

Berry Cobbler

This recipe is adapted from *Jane Brody's Good Food Book*, which is a great cookbook, although definitely not vegan. Basically this version of the cobbler has been "veganized" and adds a wonderfully decadent crumb topping. Cobbler is great when you have a lot of berries or other fruit around and are yearning for pie, but you don't want to spend hours making it. Since cobbler doesn't have a crust, it goes together really quickly.

Ingredients

⅔ cup flour

½ cup sugar

1-½ teaspoon baking powder

¼ tsp salt

⅔ cup soy milk

2 tablespoons vegan margarine, melted

2+ cups raspberries, other berries, or fruit

½ cup flour

¼ cup brown sugar

2 tablespoons butter or margarine

1. Preheat oven to 350 degrees. To prepare batter, in a medium bowl, combine ⅔ cup flour, sugar, baking powder and salt. Stir in milk and mix until smooth.

2. To prepare the crumb topping, stir flour and brown sugar together in small bowl. Cut in unmelted margarine with pastry cutter or knife until mixture is crumbly.

3. Pour melted butter into the bottom of a 1 or 1-½ quart casserole dish. Pour in batter. Sprinkle raspberries on top. Sprinkle crumb topping on raspberries.

4. Bake for 40-45 minutes until top is golden.

Index

Quick Vegan Stuffing 72

R

S

About the Authors

Susan Daffron and James Byrd have been happily and healthily vegan since 1994. They own Logical Expressions, Inc., a company that produces books, software, and online publications.

About Susan Daffron

Susan Daffron is the President of Logical Expressions, Inc. and has written more than 70 articles that have appeared in national magazines, more than 200 newspaper articles, an online software training course, a software book, and book chapters. In addition to her writing experience, Susan has more than 15 years of experience as a writer, editor, and designer of magazines, newsletters, books and other book-length documents such as users guides and manuals.

About James Byrd

James Byrd has been a programmer since 1985 and has written for numerous trade magazines and Web sites. He has experience in developing software for a wide variety of platforms from mainframes to personal computers. Before returning full time to Logical Expressions, he was a Senior Internet Developer and then Internet Development Manager for a $100 million web site (and several back-end systems) at women's clothing retailer Coldwater Creek.

Susan and James operate Logical Expressions, Inc. from their log home in North Idaho, with moral support from their four dogs and two cats.

For more information, please visit the Logical Expressions Web site at:

http://www.logicalexpressions.com

Share *Vegan Success* with a Friend

If you like this book, share the joy of vegan cooking with your friends!

Order Form

Please send me:

Qty	Title	Price	Total
	Vegan Success - Scrumptious, Healthy Vegan Recipes for Busy People	$19.95	
	Shipping & Handling - $4.50 for first book, $1.00 for each additional book for US Priority Mail within the U.S.*		

_____ Check enclosed with order

_____ Please charge my credit card [ ] Visa   [ ] Master Card

Number: _____

Name on Card: _____ Exp. Date: _____

Buyer's Name:_____

Buyer's Address: _____

Shipping Address (if different):_____

_____

Please fax to 208-265-0956 or mail order form with your payment to:

Logical Expressions, Inc.
311 Fox Glen Rd.
Sandpoint, ID 83864

* *Please contact us for more information on orders mailed outside of the U.S.*
  (Our number is 208-265-6147)